SYLVIA PLATH

A BEGINNER'S GUIDE

GINA WISKER

Series Editors
Rob Abbott & Charlie Bell

Hodder & Stoughton

A MEMBER OF THE HODDER HEADLINE GROUP

56361

Orders: please contact Bookpoint Ltd, 39 Milton Park, Abingdon, Oxon OX14 4TD. Telephone: (44) 01235 400400, Fax: (44) 01235 400500. Lines are open from 9.00–6.00, Monday to Saturday, with a 24-hour message answering service. Email address: orders@bookpoint.co.uk

British Library Cataloguing in Publication Data
A catalogue record for this title is available from The British Library

ISBN 0 340 80040 2

First published 2001
Impression number   10 9 8 7 6 5 4 3 2 1
Year 2005 2004 2003 2002 2001

Cover image supplied by Corbis.
Illustrations by Steve Coots.
Typeset by Transet Limited, Coventry, England.
Printed in Great Britain for Hodder & Stoughton Educational, a division of Hodder Headline Plc, 338 Euston Road, London NW1 3BH by Cox & Wyman, Reading, Berks.

CONTENTS

How to use this book

The *Beginner's Guide* series aims to introduce readers to the major writers of the past 500 years. It is assumed that readers will begin with little or no knowledge and will want to go on to explore the subject in other ways.

BEGIN READING THE AUTHOR

This book is a companion guide to Sylvia Plath's major works, it is not a substitute for reading the books themselves. It would be useful if you read Sylvia Plath's collected poems in parallel, so that you can put theory into practice. This book is divided into sections. After considering how to approach the author's work and a brief biography, we go on to explore some of the main writings and themes before examining some critical approaches to the author. The survey finishes with suggestions for further reading and possible areas of further study.

HOW TO APPROACH UNFAMILIAR OR DIFFICULT TEXTS

Coming across a new writer may seem daunting, but do not be put off. The trick is to persevere. Much good writing is multi-layered and complex. It is precisely this diversity and complexity that makes literature rewarding and exhilarating.

Literature often needs to be read more than once and in different ways. These ways can include: a leisurely and superficial reading to get the main ideas and narrative; a slower more detailed reading focusing on the nuances of the text, concentrating on what appear to be key passages; and reading in a random way, moving back and forth through the text to examine such things as themes or narrative or characterization. Every reader has an individual approach but undoubtedly the best way to extract the most from a text is to read it several times.

In complex texts it may be necessary to read in short chunks. When it comes to tackling difficult words or concepts it is often enough to guess in context on the first reading, making a more detailed study using a dictionary or book of critical concepts on later reading. If you prefer to look up unusual words as you go along, be careful that you do not disrupt the flow of the text and your concentration.

VOCABULARY

You will see that keywords are set in **bold** text. These words are defined and explained in the glossary to be found at the back of the book. In order to help you further we have also included a summary of each section.

You can read this introductory guide in its entirety or dip in wherever suits you. You can read it in any order. It is a tool to help you appreciate a key figure in literature. We hope you enjoy reading it and find it useful.

✳✳✳✳SUMMARY ✳✳✳✳

To maximise the use of this book:

- Read the author's work.

- Read it several times in different ways.

- Be open to innovative or unusual forms of writing.

- Persevere.

Rob Abbott and Charlie Bell

Why read Plath today?

MORE THAN THE MYTH

The myth and legend of Sylvia Plath's poetry seems to precede our reading of her. Certainly her poetry has been seen as difficult because it is complex, but its treatment of identity and relationships, its beautiful imagery and her capture of the spoken voice of a whole host of people brings it to life for us. This is energetic, mythical work. Sylvia Plath's interests in identity, the self and relationships are topical today as we become daily more used to practices of counselling and psychoanalysis and as we use creative writing as self expression and therapy. But her work is not an offloading of depression, not merely confessional. In turning the personal into the political and finding the imagery and language with which to express and move beyond feelings into art, Plath has provided us with a model and a language of feelings, thoughts and emotions.

We can identify with this search for identity, which is part of most people's lives, and expressed most sensitively and poignantly in Plath's poems. We know she was a bright American poet, wife of Ted Hughes, who tragically committed suicide, leaving a stunningly original poetry collection, *Ariel*, a biographical novel, *The Bell Jar*, largely about identity and breakdown and some other work. It is important in our reading of Sylvia Plath's intense and highly innovative writing that we jettison the myth and look at the themes and the imagery, the sounds and the emotional power of her poetic expression.

SEARCH FOR IDENTITY

Sylvia Plath writes of a search for identity and particularly as a woman. Her poems are filled with raw nerves, pain and joy. Although she died in 1963, she is very much a poet of the later twentieth century. It is difficult to separate the life from the work and indeed much of the criticism of her work has centred on the way in which her poetry reflects her life, confusing the two. She writes of her own life and of life more generally, of key moments and the ways in which we deal with them (or never really deal with them).

A major focus is on her love for and loss of her father when she was nine. She had a sense of never having fully grieved, this always being overshadowed by her love for him and anger at her sense of loss. She writes of the stresses of growing up as a woman, choosing roles, of attempted suicides. She writes of love and mixed doubts, a celebration of motherhood and a recognition of the strangeness and responsibility of having and bringing up young children. For parents and children this is refreshingly candid and honest, new in its time, and we can relate to the mixed feelings she explores.

CONFESSIONAL WORK

Much of her work is called 'confessional' not because it is an emotional therapeutic outpouring, but because of the:

* careful, precise written language
* record of senses and feelings
* imagery
* power and the tensions of explorations of self
* doubts about identity and meaning in life
* examination of relationships.

Her work examines the roles women play or are expected to play – the mother, daughter, lover, spinster, slut, the mythical women of power. These are all investigated and explored, adopted, jettisoned, shown to be enabling and constraining. Hers is an early exploration of the varieties of roles expected of women and the confusions and demands this produces.

INSIGHT INTO WOMEN'S LIVES

Both men and women readers appreciate imagery which disturbs. They see in Sylvia Plath's work a deep insight into women's lives, their constraints and artifice. Plath debates and represents each of these choices, seeing the roles in those terms, parts adopted and played, seeing all women do as role play, dressed for the parts. In investigating the conflicting and constricting roles of women in her novel, short stories, diaries, letters home and above all her poems, Plath provides an early pre-feminist comment on women's lives, her own among them. She investigates and critiques mythic representations of women as Circe, as siren, as Persephone, as other powerful mythic figures and this contributes to a major trend in reinterpreting and revaluing women's lives and their configurations in myth and legend, including popular myths, pop songs and media imagery. We should read Sylvia Plath because she takes us through such an insightful, emotional journey investigating identity, relationships and women's roles.

INFLUENCES

For contemporary readers, her work is startlingly fresh in its choice of imagery, its innovative use of the speaking voice, its dealing with images representing men and women in relationships, critiquing the 'living doll', the trapped housewife and investigating the securities and insecurities of parenthood. Her investigations of the self are developed within semi-autobiographical poetry and prose. Her work has fed into the writing of a range of writers, some African American women such as Maya Angelou, South Africans such as Bessie Head, post-colonial and contemporary UK- and USA-based men and women including the Glaswegian, James Kelman, and a host of others involved in exploring the semi-fictionalised autobiographical form in diary, letter and creative writing.

Her poetry is strung powerfully and delicately together with symbols which provide a kind of system, a key into the meaning. Objects come alive: people seem like inanimate objects. With careful precision she chooses images that destabilise our sense of security and normality causing us to see the world anew. She uses rhythms and sounds, patterns and repetitions and changes and we hear the moods develop, the questions being asked and sometimes answered. The images and sounds of her poems reflect and recreate sense impressions, inner states and thoughts and feelings.

For us as readers her poetry, her imagery, symbols, sounds and the debates she airs have currency today as they will in years to come.

* * * *SUMMARY * * * *

Sylvia Plath:

- uses imagery and symbol systems as delicate precise evocations of expressions and ideas

- reflects on feelings, identity, roles, the self

- questions the roles we play and personae we adopt, especially women's roles and relationships

- investigates, dramatises and expresses the dynamics of individual identity

- writes semi-autobiographical poetry and prose, which has influenced other writers

- develops and uses a distinct 'voice', using voice rhythms and patterns to convey different moods and different people

- connects individual experiences to the social and political, to culture and to myth.

How to approach Plath's work

THE POETRY

Sylvia Plath is best known for her poetry, although she herself argued that her poems were an 'evasion from the real job of writing prose' (quoted in Ted Hughes' introduction to *Johnny Panic and the Bible of Dreams*). This chapter will look at ways of reading her poems, since many of the themes – identity, relationships, fantasy, family women's roles, appear in both as do her techniques which entail a system of symbols or metaphors, to tell a story that mixes realistic detail and fantasy.

It is useful to think about how we read poetry and focus on Plath's work through this approach because she is a very rich poet. She is technically skilful and her work lends itself to sensitive appreciation of the use of language. Like so many poets, she has some favourite themes and some preferred ways of working which, once we have become more aware of them, can help lead us into what otherwise might be a little impenetrable.

MEANING

With Plath we are never going to be able to claim that we have found the single 'correct reading' of a poem. Poetry works *with* the reader, so new readers find new patterns, new meanings, new resonances with their own lives, with history, with issues and thought processes and expressions. If this were not so, the poems would die. So you are invited to look at a variety of interpretations. If this book appears to be looking at any single reading here, it is only because this gives you a way in to develop your own reading and also because not *every* reading of a poem really springs from the poem itself.

It is a mistake to carry round a fixed set of things we want to find in poems and seem to force these readings on to poems. There is a difference between forcing a reading and bringing your own subjective readings to Plath's lines. Just as a matter of good practice, you would probably find it useful to put any reading you (or anyone else) provides for a poem through a 'reality check'. Ask yourself 'is there real evidence – images, sounds, story, themes and so on in this poem, to suggest that this reading is possible?' There is a great deal of difference between misreading (*no* evidence in the text) and a variety of readings, which we might well be encouraged to produce, where you can show, using the text, that your ideas and arguments have grown from the words and sounds rather than just from your own beliefs and preferences.

STARTING TO READ PLATH'S POEMS

There is no substitute for reading the poems – use the critics' views later. Browse a few poems, do not expect them to reveal all their meanings to you but try to read them out loud, listen to what she is saying and how she says it. Although many of us are rather daunted by poetry, you will only end up more daunted and not a little confused if you start with reading the critics.

Every word counts

We do know that Plath wrote very carefully, selecting each word as if it stood out alone, circling it in black, building up the life of each poem from the inside, from its own root, until each has its own coherence. Every word counts. There are common themes and images which she tends to use throughout the poetry. She is also concerned with the individual quality of words and the life they contain. For example, the baby's first sounds in 'Morning Song', rise like 'balloons', individuals, 'bees'. We also find that many of the earlier poems shows Plath developing different styles, trying out traditional forms, such as experimenting with Anglo-Saxon sounding poems – see the early 'Firesong' (1956):

> Sweet salts warped stem
> Of weeds we tackle towards way's rank ending

This is filled with **alliteration** or **assonance** each aiding a taut internal rhyming, and the scents and sounds of the vegetation imagery. Much of her work experiments with established techniques and forms such as 'Sonnet: to Time'.

'Spinster': an introduction

To show how a Plath poem might be approached we will look in more detail at 'Spinster'. Here, she deals with a favourite subject, the roles and constraints which apply to women. It is a tightly structured poem with patterns of images and metaphor – rock and ice – suggesting hardness, constraint and control; birdsong and litter, suggesting life but also chaos; and patterns of

KEYWORDS

Alliteration: is the repetition of the consonant, for example, 's' or 't' to gain special rhythmical or musical effects.

Assonance: is the repetition of a vowel, for example, 'ee', 'a', to produce a particular effect.

sound. She builds up from a central idea, with a scenario (garden, spring, castle) relating to those central ideas. Read 'Spinster' through a couple of times and ask yourself: What does this seem to be about?

There will not be a single meaning, but you can try to sort out some meaning – the title of a poem is usually, but by no means always, a clue to what it is about. 'Spinster' is indeed partly about a spinster – an unmarried woman, one who does not take on a conventional male/female partnership.

What might Plath be saying about this woman and her choices, her feelings, her actions?

To some extent, in reading a poem, we do look for meaning or at least patches of meaning. Sometimes this is in the shape of part or all of a story; sometimes it is opposing arguments, versions or possibilities of ways of seeing something that is offered to us. This is not necessarily what a poem is about. Critics of the school of **New Criticism** argued that meaning is *not* what we should be looking for in a poem at all and **structuralist** critics concentrated more on the form and structure of a poem rather than its meaning, arguing that we cannot and should not attempt to find meaning but look instead at how the poem 'works'.

Some people like to read poetry for the sounds, the rhyme and the rhythm, rather than the meanings. In addition, there has been a branch of poetry – sound poetry (1960s and 1970s mainly) which is constructed just for this, it is *sound* rather than readable meaning. The way

KEYWORDS

New Criticism: A movement from the 1930s to the 1960s which became academic orthodoxy. It concentrated, at least at first, on short poems and sought to consider them as self-sufficient objects, disconnected from their origin and author. The idea was to discover the ambiguities and complexities found in a poem and to seek ways of resolving them in their own terms.

Structuralism: Intellectual movement originating in France in the 1950s in the work of Levi Straus and Richard Barthes. Stresses that things cannot be under-stood in isolationg but need to be seen in a wider context.

Plath constructs her poems, the language she uses, the sounds and patterns, are very important So we need to look at *how* she writes and at the words themselves, as *well* as searching for meaning.

Look in 'Spinster' for patterns of words, such as cold, hot, hard, soft – words that provide a certain theme or focus and sounds such as hard, soft sounds, rhyme and rhythm. What kinds of words, images, patterns of reference is she using?

Rhyme occurs at the end of a line or in the middle. See if it is a full rhyme – in other words where the words have the same ending sound – or a part rhyme – where similar/ the same sounds occur in the beginnings or the middle of more than one word quite close together or of several words over a space. Spotting the full, part or half-rhyme usually sets up a sound pattern in your mind, in your ear if you read the poem out loud. Sometimes a particular rhyme recurs or partly recurs and we link the words together to find they deliberately contrast or they could each refer to something similar. Through the rhyme she is suggesting argument, themes, ideas, emotions.

A close reading of 'Spinster'

The poem starts with the words 'now this particular girl' and immediately we are into an ambiguity. The poem singles out a specific girl but we also have a sense that she is probably rather particular, choosy? If you look through the poem you can follow a story about a young girl walking with her lover, 'suitor', another rather old-fashioned word and deciding that his actions and her feelings are rather messy and disorganised; 'his gait stray uneven'. She judges him, deciding that what he has to offer is rather disorderly. All the love he seems to offer her is compared to natural images of birds and leaves but for her the leaves in autumn are 'litter' the birdsong is cacophonous 'babble'. She seems to find him, love and natural things rather disordered and irritating. Gradually she 'withdraws neatly' and shores herself up against the suitor, birds and leaves, against nature itself. In doing this she preserves a certain individuality and protectiveness, seen in images of the castle or battlements and her refusal to 'pitch' her 'five queenly wits into vulgar motley', to become disordered herself. In doing so, she also actually rejects love. The harsh 'curse', 'threat', 'fist' are kept out with power (but so is love.

Through this brief story Plath show us a woman who chooses to remain apart, her sentiments kept within controls and borders. But she also hints that there are some problems with these choices. Look at the rejection of examples of the natural world. The **Romantic** period has left us overtones in poetry suggesting comparisons between what is worthwhile and valued and what is natural. Here Plath's young woman refuses the natural and in doing so signals to us that her choices, ordered and precise though they maybe, are a kind of unnatural problem.

> **KEYWORD**
>
> Romanticism: A movement in Britain and Europe roughly between 1770 and 1848. In literary terms it expressed the self and the value of individual experience along with a strong sense of the transcendental. The motif of the movement was 'imagination' and it had a belief in the close links between man and nature. The movement is characterised by such writers as Rousseau, Wordsworth, Mary Wollstonecraft, Coleridge, Byron and Shelley.

Imagery

There is a range of imagery throughout the poem. Some images refer to order – cold, ice, frost, others to life – nature, birds, songs. Several others note the imperious and controlling, queenly and rather medieval, in terms of castles and battlements. The patterns of imagery suggest that the choice of remaining aloof and rejecting love is going against the natural. This is rather medieval, imperious. So Plath has turned courtly love images of the medieval romances on their head. This young woman rejects, using her queenly wits and in so doing chooses both to be herself and not just part of a pair but also, rather sterile, like ice and frost, deathly.

Plath's images and patterns of sound set up patterns of argument within the poem. 'Spinster' is a poem typical of much of her work because it deals with choices available to women – here, to fall in love and enter the uneven disorder, lose her identity and singleness or to choose to remain away from everything including love and so actually lose the natural. We find Plath using patterns of images and metaphors throughout the poems and also patterns of sound, for example, her assonance of 'pitch', 'wits', 'gait', which echo sounds and link together ideas.

Plath forms patterns of image and sounds, rhyme and rhythms and her poems explore issues to do with myths and representations of women and the roles open to women.

'THE APPLICANT'

In 'The Applicant' Plath explores the roles open to men and women in society and finds both very constricting. She adopts the hectoring tone of a salesman who calls in the reader/ subject/ protagonist of the poem as an applicant.

The applicant receives his doll.

On a first reading, the poem seems to be critiquing the roles offered to women, as it mentions a 'living doll' but on further reading it is more generous in gender terms, critiquing roles on offer to both men and women. Indeed, the hectoring tone of the salesman is addressing a male applicant who seems to be seeking some kind of entrance to the human race and feels some kind of initial lack. The lack is to be sorted out for him in the shape of partner or woman. The voice invites him, recognising something that is missing. Using a tone more suited to children: 'stop crying', he says, asking the applicant to open his hand. Into this he will place something or someone who will overcome headaches and all number of ordinary and everyday human problems. The woman figure will roll away headaches and complete the needs of the man (who was not aware that he had a lack). The set of domestic images refers to the prevailing stereotypical notions of women especially as portrayed in the media.

The male figure shown a female partner, has a 'living doll' fifties' version of woman offered to him who will clearly act as some kind of impossible insurance policy against 'storms through the roof' and any other complex and destructive scenarios. The linking of the offered promise of marriage with that of insurance highlights the specific cultural lie that relationships and marriage solve every problem. Coffin imagery equates the wedding suit the man will wear with a coffin itself; this black suit is 'not a bad fit' (and demonstrates a little of Plath's black humour).

By using everyday colloquial language taken from a common situation, that of a salesman, Plath draws the reader in, to involve them in the choices and offers. The sales pitch is not just about an individual transaction but about life. The young man to whom the pitch is made is being offered a way of life which includes a wife, whose mechanical elements are emphasised by the mechanical sounding images and sounds of the poem: 'it can cook it can sew, it can talk talk talk', 'marry it marry it marry it'. The man has no choice. His life is mechanically ordered for him and a partner who is an automaton is all that is on offer. In this scenario both men and women lose.

The colloquialisms of the period, its images and its problems, allow Plath to explore the kinds of constraints and ties offered to both men or women at that time.

PLATH AND TECHNIQUE

Sylvia Plath is always in touch with the tensions of the times, transmuting these through her art, making personal what is political and historical and finding the exact word and image to evoke the emotion or the argument she seeks. In an interview with Peter Orr she says:

> I think my poems come immediately out of the sensuous and emotional experiences I have, but I must say I cannot sympathise with these cries from the heart that are informed by nothing except, you know, a needle or a knife … I believe one should be able to control and manipulate experiences, even the most terrifying, like madness, like being tortured … and should be able to manipulate these experiences with an informed and intelligent mind.

You can approach both her poetry and her prose in terms of a comment on gendered roles and on her times. Hers is a careful selection of language to express choices, context, constraints and inner feelings.

✳ ✳ ✳ ✳SUMMARY ✳ ✳ ✳ ✳

Sylvia Plath's work should be appreciated for:

- the use of colloquial and appropriate tones and language

- the way she can handle and critique cultural and other myths about women, and men

- its imagery, systems of metaphors and symbols, and internal rhyme

- the patterns of reference, sound, and sense

- the translation of the personal into the topical and political.

Biography and influences 1932–1963

EARLY YEARS

Sylvia Plath was born in Boston on the October 27 1932, first child of Otto and Aurelia Plath. Otto, a professor of biology at Boston University, had come to the USA at the age of 15 from the Polish Corridor, an area now in Eastern Germany. In 1934 he published a treatise on the behaviour of bees, 'Bumblebees and their ways', and bee imagery runs throughout much of Plath's work (although this was not the only source, since she and Ted Hughes kept bees in Devon later on). Aurelia Plath's parents were Austrian and lived in Winthrop, a seaside Boston suburb. Sylvia's brother, Warren, was born in 1935. Otto contracted gangrene as a result of diabetes and his last months were spent bedridden, making moaning noises. He died when Sylvia was only eight but his life and death had an immense and lasting effect on her life, as Ted Hughes' *Birthday Letters* testify.

Sylvia was always seeking her father's approval both loving and hating him; dominated by his death and by her mother's refusal to mourn openly; and her mother's refusal to let Sylvia attend the funeral.

EARLY SUCCESS

At her father's death they moved from the coast, to Wellesley, a mostly comfortable Boston suburb. In 1950 Sylvia graduated from high school and won a part scholarship to prestigious Smith College, funded by Olive Higgins Prouty, a popular novelist. Plath was gifted, competitive and prolific in her writing. She published her first short story, 'And summer will not come again', in *Seventeen* magazine and a poem 'Bitter Strawberries' in the *Christian Science* monitor. Other poems and short stories followed. In 1953 she won a fiction contest sponsored by *Mademoiselle* magazine, working as a guest editor representing Smith College for a month in the summer, an event recorded in *The Bell Jar*.

THE GIRL WHO WOULD BE GOD

Plath's life was always one of extreme elation and success, drive and ambition to write well, interlaced with periods of self-doubt and depression. Rejected from Frank O'Connor's writing class in 1953 and exhausted, she swallowed a bottle of sleeping pills and was hospitalised for her suicide attempt. This period of hospitalisation and breakdown forms a major element in *The Bell Jar* where Esther's mother on a visit suggests the suicide could be taken as only a bad dream. 'The world in itself is the bad dream' notes Esther: 'I remembered everything' (Chapter 20).

The Journals of Sylvia Plath (1982, USA) end in 1959 and a new edition (2000) *The Journals of Sylvia Plath 1950–1962* adds much more detail to what we know of her last years and from *Letters Home: Correspondence 1950–1963* (1975). These journals give us a sense of a young woman striving to be perfect in every way possible but also aware of the constraints and contradictions of her gendered role. An early journal entry (at around age 16) has her stating that she wants to be great, 'The Girl who would be God?'

Her desire to be a perfect writer and a perfect woman, successful in many ways, has been seen as a set of constrictions and contradictions which beset many women in the 1950s. Comparisons between the two famous suicides, Plath and Marilyn Monroe, have focused on this. However, this is also the driving manifesto of a young, ambitious woman with a mother who focused on her daughter's success, who internalised and developed this drive for herself. In 1948 she wrote of her own drive to write:

> You ask me why I spend my life writing?
> Do I find entertainment?
> Is it worthwhile?
> Above all, does it pay?
> If not, then is there a reason?
> I write only because
> there is a voice within me
> that will not be still

ENGLAND

After returning to Smith and winning several poetry competitions, Plath graduated and won a Fulbright Scholarship to Cambridge. 1955 is a transitional year. Plath moved from the USA to the UK and saw this as a period of finding her voice, achieving opportunities and trying new worlds. Her poem 'The Princess and the Goblins' suggests such change, seeing a 'wakeful princess' climbing a spiral stair then a 'visionary ladder towards the moon/ whose holy blue anoints her injured hand' (p.333). The change is seen as growth, a fruitful development for writing.

In Cambridge, Plath was 'an American abroad', seeing the place in a new light, measuring herself against its opportunities and its English constrictions. She noted the eccentricities of the women dons – Dickensian, grotesque – and wrote of the beauties and hidden threats of Grantchester meadows – a critique of the English maintenance of 'face' and its hiding of cruelty. Contradictory versions of Sylvia also appear when we see her posing in the pages of the Cambridge University magazine *Varsity* wearing various polka dot swimsuits. Great scholar and aspiring writer, she also expressed women's performativity – dressed in fashion, seeking a partner who would be an Adam to her Eve. Her first meetings with Ted Hughes produced such images. In 'Ode to Ted', she talks of being 'Adam's woman'.

TED HUGHES

Plath met Ted Hughes in February 1956 when she joined a poetry group which he and a friend 'led'. Her *Journal* records the event in terms of action, nature and noise. 'We shouted as if in a high wind', 'I stamped and screamed'. He was, she wrote to her mother, the only man she felt 'was strong enough for her'. He was also an increasingly popular and famous poet and certainly one of Sylvia Plath's main aims was to support him in his success while, herself more minor and younger, she worked on at her own poetry. They married in June 1956. Her sense of the achievement of unity and endless possibilities of writing growing from this appears in 'Wreath for a Bridal' when she says 'let flesh be knit and each step hence go famous'.

Plath helped Hughes find an American audience and Hughes helped Plath find an English one when, after her death, he edited her work. This last supportive and selective activity has been the subject of much controversy as Hughes left out some elements and poems; the more intimate and the nastier. He organised the last poems and collected poems in a certain order which was not that left by Plath herself. However, although the various factions who rage around the two poets have variously supported and denounced this choice, Hughes latterly explained that Plath's writing processes constantly regrouped the poems in different orders and it would be difficult to decide exactly which she had finally wanted. His editing, he argues, was largely to protect the children and friends, as well as Plath herself.

AMERICA AND BACK

In the spring of 1957, Plath and Hughes moved back to the USA and lived in Cape Cod in the summer, moving to Smith College in the autumn, where Sylvia began to teach. They both found the trials of teaching and writing too contradictory and decided to write full time, which they did from 1958, living first in Boston, travelling the USA and then coming back to England in December 1959, moving between the two countries for a few years. They moved from Yorkshire to London in February 1960 and Sylvia gained her first book contract for *The Colossus*, signing her letter to her mother and Warren 'your authoress' (February 11, 1960).

MOTHERHOOD

Her daughter, Frieda, was born on April 1 1960 and it was a few months before she started writing again, managing a baby and a household. The following year Plath had both a miscarriage and her appendix removed, which gave her a period in hospital observing others – one woman entirely in plaster. Joan (probably) appears in the poem 'In Plaster' which records a sense of alienation between mind and body. For Plath this is also the period during which she was writing *The Bell Jar*, her autobiographical novel. In this Esther shows a disgust for dead babies in pickling jars which probably derives from Plath's own miscarriage and hospitalisation. Esther's attempted suicide and

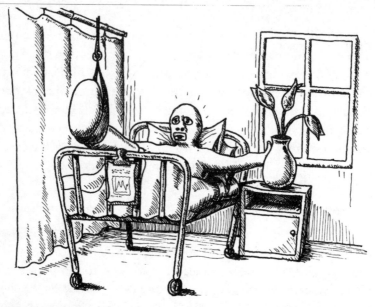

Plath wrote about her experiences.

the process of recovery re-awoke memories in Plath at a difficult time and she uses images of shipwreck, white bandages, herself a 'thirty year old cargo boat', hanging onto a past which others are 'swabbing clean of living associations' ('Tulips', March 1961). In January 1962 their son Nicholas was born. Her letters reveal her happiness in motherhood and her involvement in the local Devon community. Bee keeping was a feature of this period and appears as a motif in her poetry.

Sylvia Plath's discovery that Hughes was having an affair with family friend Alessia Wevill during his increasingly lengthy periods in London, led to a series of bitter, angry poems. She had dedicated herself to the achievement of several key roles and ideals – great poet and writer, great wife and mother. Many critics have seen the tensions in these conflicting roles becoming too great for her at this time. Maybe her expectations were too great; certainly her obsessional nature drove her to write great poetry. Yet maybe also the myth of the doomed woman poet hangs over our interpretations of Plath's anguish and her then period of rapid, stunning writing, (which emerges posthumously as *Ariel*), followed by her suicide.

Her life and achievement pre-date mid-twentieth-century feminism. Plath seems to have been without such politically engaged women friends. She had no model and no forum for dealing with the contradictions of the time. Her poetry shows her anger. In 'The Other', July 2 1962 she writes of:

> Sulfurous adulteries grieve in a dream.
> Cold glass, how you insert yourself

('The Other' p.202)

LONDON

'Words Heard by Accident, Over the Phone', on July 11 1962, reflects anger at the deception, in its title, emphasised further in the language of the poem: 'a hiss', 'tentacle'. She moved to London, finding a flat in what was once the poet W.B. Yeats' house and settled down to write and bring up her two children. But the letters home at this period testify to the intense cold and the dreariness of an English winter. After her mother's visit in 1962, they also become more honest about her suffering from the loss of her one big love.

DEPRESSION AND DEATH

Sylvia turned her anguish into a writing burst, but a house full of wet nappies and babies and an intense period of writing in the early hours of the morning, produced tensions and exhaustion which emerge as contradictory behaviour in her letters and the memories people have of her at this time. Sometimes she was elated, sometimes depressed, all perfectly natural given the circumstances of her life.

Speculation surrounds her death on February 11 1963. The death was contributed to by tablets taken to control depression, by absences and bad luck. Sylvia Plath left a note for the doctor, called a babysitter and left her children sleeping, then gassed herself. The babysitter, arriving at her door and unable to gain entry, joined a queue to phone and check the address with her agency and, on return, was too late, while Sylvia Plath's doctor neighbour probably slept through knocks at their shared building door as the gas had travelled through the building and partly affected *his* flat.

It could be argued that the suicide was a cry for help, as are many suicides. It is also part of a personal mythology and pattern, her sense of rising anew from the ashes of an old life, like a phoenix, which appears in 'Lady Lazarus' when she charts her suicide attempts and in a wildly Romantic gesture, she (falsely) sees even death as an art she can control and live through:

Dying
Is an art, like everything else.
I do it exceptionally well

....

What follows is a phoenix-like renewal:

Out of the ash
I rise with my red hair
And I eat men like air.

('Lady Lazarus', pp.244–7)

Ted Hughes comments of her that she was too dangerously close to her art and 'she had none of the usual guards and remote controls to protect herself from her own reality – she lived right in it, especially during the last two years of her'. Her work has 'a common identity of active self and poetic genius' (Introduction to *Collected Poems*, 1981).

Who knows how her poems would have developed beyond this brief and intense period of her writing, had she lived. Her friend, the poet Anne Sexton, says, 'Never mind last diggings, they don't matter. What matters is her poems. These last poems stun me, they eat time.'

And her work has outlasted her. Although Ted Hughes has been demonised by many, most particularly by feminist critics following Plath's death, nonetheless he edited her work and had it published. Latterly, in his publication of the *Birthday Letters* (Faber, 1999), he broke the silence about his own sense of being caught up in her scenario. Honestly and generously he celebrates her intensity, their love, her loss.

* * * *SUMMARY * * * *

- Plath transmuted her life into her art.
- Her relationship with Ted Hughes was formative, supportive and, ultimately, destructive.

4 Major themes

INFLUENCES

Plath did not work in total isolation. She has many American influences, notably the confessional poet Robert Lowell, whose poetry classes she attended with her friend Anne Sexton, also an influence on Plath's work – as was Plath on hers. We can see traces of the metaphysical and the personal soul searching and the imagery and flow of other 'American Greats' such as Emily Dickinson. Her early work is influenced by Theodore Roethke and the imagery of Pablo Neruda, the Peruvian poet. Modernist T.S. Eliot can also be traced with his concentration on imagism, the perfect capturing of a thought or expression in a carefully wrought image and his sounds of coastal America.

The greatest single influence on her writing was certainly Ted Hughes, although had she lived beyond the winter of 1962/3 other influences might well have changed the course of the way she wrote. Margaret Uroff, the critic who has written of both poets together, rejects the notion of Plath as passive victim and sees the Hughes/ Plath marriage and writing relationship as symbiotic, each drawing from and supporting the other. When we look at their work we see different traditions – Hughes a British, Anglo Saxon metre, focusing on nature, Plath the more confessional, American, often highly wrought with a concentration on perfectly honed phrase and image. Together their work shows them 'rehearsing and developing together parts of a continuing debate about the nature of the universe, in which Plath's reservations and Hughes' assertions play against each other' (*Sylvia Plath and Ted Hughes*, University of Illinois Press, Chicago and London, 1979).

REPRESENTING A LIFE

In looking at the ways in which Plath deals with her identity and relationships, we are necessarily involved in how she represents her own life. The autobiographical reading of her work is a very popular one and one troubled by us bringing our own critical and personal concerns into interpretations of her work. Plath's work deals with gender roles and with the responsibilities and practices of writing.

ROLES FOR WOMEN

Plath spent much of her time when writing poetry concentrating on forming a sense of identity constructed in relation to the roles offered to women, in society. For example in 'Two Sisters of Persephone', the speaker is clearly dealing with the roles offered to women but her choices are actually very limited. There seems only the two roles available: on the one hand, women can be cold, sterile and unable to produce children. For Plath's speaker, it is not a positive choice but rather an issue of loss. The other choice is that of excessive fecundity, blooming, productive, rich and fertile. This woman becomes a kind of earth mother but she is also seen as a mindlessly fertile creature. Here Plath can be seen working out historically positioned tensions in women's roles.

A duality of roles

One woman sits in a 'dark wainscoted room' working out sums. Her life also a 'mathematical machine', she goes squint-eyed, 'rat-shrewd', her body is 'meagre', 'root-pale', her enterprise 'barren' although she is clearly highly organised and ordered. The other, meanwhile, lies in the sun, an earth mother/goddess figure sucked into the earth's life, mindless, fruitful. 'Bronzed as earth' she is 'Lulled/near a bed of poppies' but goes on to become pregnant, 'earthily, with seed' and to become a mother, to a 'king'. The calculating, shrewd, cold spinster however, marries only death, represented in an echo of Marvell's 'To his Coy Mistress', where the speaker, trying to seduce a women, says only the worms will try her virginity when she is dead. So Plath's barren woman is a 'wry virgin' who:

Goes graveward, with flesh laid waste,
Worm-husbanded, yet no woman.

('Two Sisters of Persephone')

There seems to be little space for the woman artist in either scenario but certainly the choices between producing children or not are clearly shown. There is no space here for joyful choices of remaining unmarried: this speaker can only see a terrible waste, a frightening sterility. Many readers have (in more recent years after the second wave of feminism in the 1970s) found this limited perception of polarised roles of women rather irritating, but it was certainly a topical issue for women in the post-war 1950s, Plath's period of growing up into a woman.

The witch

The poem that follows 'Two Sisters of Persephone' in the *Collected Poems* represents another version of women's choices and lives and of the social and mythical compulsions driving women's roles. 'Vanity Fair' references marriage to the King of the Underworld. In classical mythology this was the fate of Persephone kidnapped and taken below the earth for six months of the year – our winter. It uses gothic imagery to present a calculating witch (another female stereotype – the hunted and destroyed outsider) frost, ravens, crows (crow's feet suggesting ageing as well as rooks and ravens, the birds who mythically signify death) stains, cutting and cooking images, 'heart's oven', 'cook batter', knife. Images of cooking, devouring and spell-casting are interwoven, suggesting a link between the desire to marry and cook for a husband, dangerous complicity in fatal activities under the will of the witch and being devoured, sacrificed as 'the sun hosts soul up after the lids fatal shut'. Giving up everything to the 'black king', Satan, each girl:

Vies with best queen over
Right to blaze as satan's wife;
Housed in earth, those million brides shriek out.
Some burn short, some long,
Staked in pride's coven.

('Vanity Fair')

Fulfilment as a wife

Marriage is also seen as a rich fulfilment. In looking at the whole of Plath's work we do not see a single forced version but rather an exploration of paradoxes, of alternatives worked through in mythic fairytale and topically social examples. Celebrating marriage at the time of her own wedding, Plath wrote in 'Wreath for a Bridal', of a unity and celebration blessed by natural imagery and religion. Green leaves, owls, birds, animals and a 'thresh of wings' celebrate their partnership, while words such as 'surpliced', 'cloistered', 'witness', 'bedded like angels', relate marriage with the heavenly and the sanctified. Images of unity and fecundity, of children, fruit and flowers, a rejection of mythic figures such as dragons, echo the imagery of **Spenser's** 'Epithalamion'. They go off into their world and future, unified and blessed, a perfect creative partnership:

KEYWORD

Edmund **Spenser** was a poet writing during the time of Queen Elizabeth I. 'Epithalamion' was a bridal celebration.

Let flesh be knit, and each step hence go famous.

('Wreath for a Bridal', pp. 44–5)

The widow

Plath also investigates the role of the widow and of the wronged wife. 'The Widow' operates on networks and repetitions of words related to death, loneliness, emptiness and lack of communication. Plath explores absences and the lack / loss of identity and meaning that accompany the losing of a husband. The word 'Widow' is repeated, starting five of the eight stanzas, followed by definitions and scenarios.

There are constant suggestions of the absence of the partner, shown even in the emptiness of one hand holding the lack of another's hand: 'Hand folding hand, and nothing in between.' Although the paper of the word burning in the fire turns to the paper of his letters to her held against her heart, his absence terrifies. It is suggested she fears his soul might pointlessly be trying to reach her, like a bird beating against a pane of glass, unheard, only looking on and a ghost, unable to join in.

The strumpet

The strumpet sees her own reflection.

The early poems focus on a search for identity as a woman and a poet, but much of the search is filled with images of contradiction and paradox. One possible self she recognises in 'Strumpet Song' is the strumpet, hounded and harmed by the village. Seeing the strumpet to be a version of self is a moment of clarifying identity, but also a moment of threat and loss.

Hidden identity

Plath's endless search for perfection brought many versions of self into conflict. Plath writes about a search for identity and writes about her life and its contradictions. She transmutes this into art and articulates it through networks and patterns of images and symbols that recur and develop through linked patterns of sound and reference within and between her poems and prose works. Artists typically take a search for an expression of identity as a key theme, and here Plath is no exception, but it is not a straightforward **Bildungsroman** or story of her developing life and her actions. It is an artistically formed set of explorations of what could have happened, what could happen, what happens to them and how she manages to steer a path between her own feelings and experiences and these diverse alternatives.

KEYWORD

Bildungsroman: A German originated word, used to mean the story of an individual's life. Famous examples in fiction are *Jane Eyre, Oliver Twist, Portrait of the Artist as a Young Man.*

The trapped woman

Sandra M. Gilbert notes the concentration on an enclosed, hidden identity which needs to break out and a set of contradictory identities, some hidden, some performing for the word, a common theme in Plath:

> Being enclosed – in plaster, in a bell jar, a cellar or a wax-house – and then being liberated from an enclosure by a maddened suicidal or 'hairy and ugly' avatar of the self is, I would contend, the heart of the myth that we piece together from Plath's poetry, fiction, and life.
>
> (Sandra Gilbert 'A Fine White Flying Myth: The Life/Work of Sylvia Plath' in *Shakespeare's Sisters* ed. Gilbert and Gubar Bloomington: Indiana University Press, 1979)

In this she compares Plath's work to that of several other nineteenth- and twentieth-century women writers, citing Charlotte Bronte's *Jane Eyre* in which Bertha Mason, the mad Creole alter ego of Jane, is kept in an attic. Gilbert and Gubar's *The Madwoman in the Attic*, focuses on fictions of trapped women, of versions of the woman as incarcerated, her sexual energies locked up and socially denied, her self imprisoned by society and then, often, escaping or trying to escape.

The foetal woman and the queen bee

In her bee-keeping poems, Plath also explores images of the self as a queen bee – important, protected, fecund, fatal to the drone she picks out as her mate and finally trapped in her own fecundity within the hive. In 'Stings' she writes of the queen bee 'now she is flying' emphasising her powers and her escape – in death:

> More terrible than she ever was, red
> Scar in the sky, red comet
> Over the engine that killed her –
> The mausoleum, the wax house.

('Stings', p.215)

Women's achievement of identity and power, this suggests, could also be a death sentence. 'In Plaster' concentrates on establishing a sense of an inner identity set against the alternative of an external, **performative**, acceptable, pure white, perfect (plaster, eternal) self. It begins:

> **KEYWORD**
>
> Performative: Where the language used actually performs the deed to which it refers. In Plath's case, where she explores the 'performances' required by women's roles through the language which describes it.

> I shall never get out of this! There are two of me now:
> This new absolutely white person and the old yellow one,

('In Plaster', p.158)

The whiteness, the 'tidiness', calmness and perfection of the white cast of the plaster, its saint-like self, has only been given an identity by the yellow inner hidden self, which is then described as a 'half corpse' and against the plotting external self. The plaster support is a cast that, like a mummy's eternal cast, she wishes, she claims, to take her over, as a version of the self. The relationship is compared to 'a kind of marriage, being so close' but doomed because of contradictory versions of self, vying for superiority. The split self cannot go on. The performative version in the word has to relinquish its control:

> I used to think we might make a go of it together –
> After all, it was kind of marriage, being so close.
> Now I see it must be on or the other of us.
> She may be a saint, and I may be ugly and hairy,

('In Plaster')

FREEDOM, FLIGHT AND FEAR

In the bee poems the speaker expresses a desire for freedom and flight and a fear that such a flight, an escape, is also a death. This is also echoed in the poem 'Ariel' which give its name to her greatest collection, written just prior to her death. Dragged to life, removed from death wraps, she escapes but it is into a freedom which could also be death: 'I /am the arrow,/ the dew that lies/ Suicidal, at one with the dive/ Into the red/ Eye, the cauldron of morning.'

The debate about roles, relationships and freedoms runs throughout Plath's work, as she strives through her speakers to suggest that individuality can both take flight, but also be confined, pinned down, through the lifecycle, through relationships, home, history, roles. The artist needs to fly the roles but she is tied down and a person. The tensions run throughout.

FAMILY AND RELATIONSHIPS

Sylvia Plath wrote complex poems about family relationships which frequently call on mythic references *and* which suggest universally recognisable scenarios. She writes about her relationship with her father, throughout her work. 'The Colossus' recalls his memory, the power he has had over her imagination and her life and the sense of loss which followed his death. In this poem Plath sees her father as if he were a part of the establishment and figures him as an ancient construction, the Colossus of Rhodes. The sense that he has knowledge she would like to seek for herself appears when she says he is an 'oracle' and she would like to 'dredge the silt from your throat'. Her father's death left her with one dominant memory. Never allowed to mourn him formally, Plath brought him into her poetry and prose all her life. 'Daddy' (see Chapter 5) explores the tension between love/hate resulting from each psychic dimension.

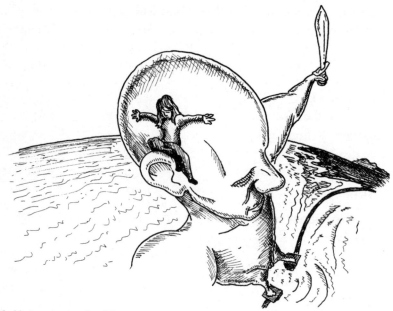

Plath's poems were her life.

WRITING AND PROCREATION/DEATH

Her intention of becoming a good mother is evident early in her journals when she states (*Journals*, 1957, p.166):

> I will write until I begin to speak my deep self, and then have children and speak still deeper. The life of the creative mind first, and then the creative body.

Poetry for her is a creative act on a par with childbirth and childrearing and she wishes to achieve perfection in all three. There are several poems about children and motherhood: 'Metaphors', 'You're', 'Morning Song', and 'Nick and the Candlestick'. Plath also wrote a verse play for the radio, 'Three Women' which investigates childbirth, miscarriage and the loss of a child.

The play was written for Radio Solent in May 1962 and broadcast on the Third Programme on September 13 1962. It is set in a maternity ward where three women lie. One, the Girl, longs for a child, giving birth to a 'red, terrible girl'. Another, the Secretary, whose life, like her office, is flat, mechanical, filled with 'black keys', is bled white, wax-like. And a third, the Wife, centre 'of a monstrosity' has a 'blue, furious boy'. The ward is white, the sheets white, the bed is compared with a cold white wing of a swan. The place seems sterile and against it is described as a 'garden of black and red agonies'. Each woman is entirely separate, echoed in the form which interleaves three separate monologues. After their experiences, each woman considers how to live on, their lives changed – emptied or overfull. The Wife feels thoroughly fulfilled after such extreme pain:

> What did my fingers feel before they held him?
> What did my heart do, with its love?
> I have never seen a thing so clear.
> His lids are like the lilac-flower
> And soft as a moth, his breath.
> I shall not let go.
> There is no guile or warp in him. May he keep so.

The Secretary suffers a miscarriage. She sees the world and herself through images of the moon, winter, emptiness and flatness. The third character, the Girl, who leaves behind her child, feels flatness, a loss she cannot name: 'What is it I miss?' Plath investigates three different scenarios in the maternity ward. Her poetic play shows intense insight into the pain, gains and losses of pregnancy and birth.

'Stillborn'

Her poem 'Stillborn' explicitly relates the creation of poems directly to the creation of children. In this case the flaws of the stillborn child parallel those of a poem that also fails to 'live' or properly take shape: 'These poems do not live.' The poem begins relating each element of a stillborn child, forehead, fingers and toes, to the processes of writing a poem that has not come to life. The stillborn baby's large misformed forehead bulges with concentration, recalling the concentrating of the poet writing a poem. Like a perfect, dead child sitting in pickling fluid, the number and parts of the poem are also perfect, but it has no life of its own. The frustration and loss felt by the mother at her dead child is paralleled by that of the poet whose fully formed poem seems to lack her voice, to finally to come to life:

> But they are dead, and their mother near dead with distraction,
> And they stupidly stare, and do not speak of her.

> ('Stillborn', p.142)

The image of stillborn children recurs in *The Bell Jar* when Buddy, the medical student, takes Esther to see unborn foetuses in jars, horrifying her.

STERILITY

In the harsh 'Munich Mannequins', Plath explicitly links sterility with the inhuman. The inviolate nature of the childless woman is frightening, perfect, but purposeless:

> Perfection is terrible, it cannot have children.
> Cold as snow breath, it tamps the womb
>
> Where the yew trees blow like hydras,
> The tree of life and the tree of life
>
> Unloosing their moons, month after month, to no purpose.

> ('Munich Mannequins', pp.262–3)

This poem aligns the horror of childlessness with the yew tree, a symbol of death, and refers (moons – monthly repetition) to menstruation, women's cycle aligned with the natural, here unfulfilled and, thus, terrible in her eyes.

CELEBRATION

There are also some celebratory poems of childbirth and childrearing. 'Nick and the Candlestick' is one of the most interesting and least accessible in its imagery. The speaker visits the child at night with a candle and this evokes images of mining, the womb like a cave, producing the child, her candlelight producing a reflection which is fishlike, recalling the shape of the child in the womb. As the 'piranha/religion' drinks from her, so the candle stutters and reclaims itself and the boy, it is suggested, drinks.

The most positive of the childbirth and mothering poems is 'Morning Song' which begins on a celebratory note, matching the moment of conception with that of reward for long service, the gold watch ticking like the baby's heart: 'Love set you going like a fat gold watch.'

Plath was a caring mother.

This is not a conventionally 'cute' poem about babies. And it is the more realistic for that, representing the arrival of the child as a desired event, but surprising; the child both an immense responsibility and yet an individual being, separate from the older parents. The individuality and the newness of the child are emphasised in the images of the museum, the parents standing around 'blankly like walls'. If this seems a little alienating, the verses that follow change the tone to one of instinct and care. The speaker hears a 'far sea' in her ear, an instinctive sound, like that we hear when raising a shell to our ears, something eternal and linking us to nature. At this sound, without thought, she stumbles from her bed 'cow heavy and floral/ in my Victorian nightgown', the voluminous gown suggesting history and a Laura Ashley kind of earth mother whose child lies in a room in a cot with walls papered in 'flat pink roses'. The child instinctively swallows the milk its mother gives, compared to a cat swallowing milk: 'Your mouth opens clean as a cat's' and the window, as dawn comes up, 'swallows its dull stars'. Agelessness, instinct and nature all relate to the care of the child which asserts itself as an individual joining the human race trying out its new sounds: 'The clear vowels rise like balloons.' This final image is a celebratory one, an individual loosed upon the world, a reminder of children's parties.

✳ ✳ ✳✳SUMMARY ✳ ✳ ✳ ✳

Major themes in the work of Sylvia Plath include:

- identity and self; being in the world – sense of relativity and oneness

- relationships: family love, male and female relationships, mothering, the relationship with her father

- roles for men and for women in society – their contrasts, the myths surrounding them

- the responsibilities and actions of a writer: conflicts or problems between the role of being a woman and that of being a writer.

Major works: the poetry

5

'The bloodjet is poetry: there is no stopping it.'

Our reading of Sylvia Plath's writing is as filled with rich and fascinating paradoxes as is the work itself. Technically accomplished, an American Fulbright scholar and 'golden girl' of the fifties' post-war generation, Plath is also represented as merely a hysterical (female) suicide whose poems are dangerously confessional, close to the edge, schizophrenic.

The contradictions of the age were hers and they appear throughout her work. Some critics argue that had she written 20 years later for instance, these kinds of contradictions might not have been present and so she might not have felt the terrible splits which so destabilise her at different points in her life. However, perhaps the poetry thrives on exploring the contradictions between cultural expectations and the individual. Certainly, her explorations of such conflicts and tensions have informed much great work by men and by women.

HORROR

In the latter years of the twentieth and early years of the twenty first century we can perhaps recognise more clearly an interest in facing up to what terrifies. Horror writers of these millennial years (Anne Rice, Stephen King, Poppy Z. Brite and others) often focus on the same areas of interest as does Plath, using similar imagery. And the humour of horror emerges in Plath's work too, something much overlooked by critics.

Sylvia Plath's major works include poetry, mostly now collected in the *Collected Poems* (Faber 1981), prose, the novel *The Bell Jar* (1963), collection of short stories *Johnny Panic and The Bible of Dreams* (1977), biographical work including the *Letters Home* (1975) to her mother, and her *Journals* (2000). Her editor, Ted Hughes, described her work as of one piece, patterns and expressions, symbols and concerns working their way through poetry and prose alike, connecting, building on previous references, working out problems and issues. Her work returns to recurring memories, fantasies and fears, pulling together ideas and thoughts, working things out from different angles and in different forms – short stories, novel, conventionally formed poems, (for example a sonnet, regular rhyme) or more innovative poetry.

JUVENILIA

In her *Collected Poems*, Plath's pre-1956 work appears under the collected title 'Juvenilia'. Some were class assignments for her professor at Smith College, Alfred Young Fisher, who made editorial comments and suggestions which she followed. Her interest in the political historical moment emerges in 'Bitter Strawberries' where girls picking strawberries in a field discuss the Russians, war, death and the draft, one girl pleading that they stop saying things like 'bomb them off the map', while another symbolically snaps the strawberry from its stem.

There are poems about family roles in 'Family Reunion' and a consistent theme of working out responses to love, men and to the roles women must negotiate, often seen as contradictory, daring, threatening, destructive. In 'Song for a Revolutionary Love' making their love anew in an honest form is a necessity set against contemporary images of nuclear war and holocaust, products of a controlling patriarchal system: 'Undo the doings of the fathering age/chuck the broken acropolis out' and:

> Then hurl the bare world like a bluegreen ball
> back into the holocaust
> to burn away the humbug rust
> and again together begin it all.

> ('Song for a Revolutionary Love', p.323)

Plath's colloquial turn of phrase, the accessible language, mixes interestingly together with a set of historical and mythical references. The Acropolis in Athens is a grand testimony to past ages of power. However, like the 'seven wonders' of the world, their time is over, they are remains only. The disruptive, energetic newness of this love and unity sets itself against the tricks and deceptions of a past age.

GENDER ROLES

Several poems represent the imaginative, creative, woman negotiating love, everyday life, contradictions and opportunities as if a circus performer. These images emphasise the performativity, the **constructedness** of gendered roles: how women and men adopt socially constructed roles in order to act out what being male or female seems to demand in our society. The performance is both energetically entered into with skill and seen as something which could take you over, consume you, threatening because it could become all you are – just a role. Performance highlights insecurities of identity. Plath debates roles and opportunities for women, closely tied up with her thoughts about her developing individual identity, and her opportunities and possibilities as a woman writer. In 'Trio of Love Songs', she is an 'acrobat', her love 'more athletic than a verb' but her daring in love, like her daring in language, are linked, both exciting and vulnerable: they might not come through:

> **KEYWORD**
>
> Constructedness: refers to the socially prescribed nature of meanings that are placed on words and concepts. Women's roles are seen to be constructed because they are what society has imposed.

Treading circus tightropes
of each syllable,
the brazen jackanapes
would fracture if he fell.

('Trio of Love Songs')

'Circus in Three Rings' uses images of magicians, Mephistopheles, demons, trapezes as she claims to control her love like a ringmistress ('yet I flourish my whip with a fatal flair), 'eclipsed' by the powerful male magician whose tricks, devilish, could make everything vanish, leaving her with 'a smoke that clears my eyes'. Love is dangerous. Images of death, power and magic unite with those of performance, and the sado-masochistic undertones (whips, wounds, gnawings of love) run throughout. Here Plath establishes some of the concerns and images she uses throughout her work which combine the theatrical and the imaginative/ fantastic, the mythical, performative and the everyday to deal with love, relationships, self, identity, mothering and gender roles. Balancing versions of what it means to be a woman and what it means to be a writer is like walking a tightrope. In 'Aerialist' the talented tightrope walker survives attacks from jealous males who would force their power and their version of her upon her (she should be more submissive, they insist). In a rather sexual image, her body is taken nightly, by dream into the circus to perform feats, commanded by a master.

Applause is contrasted with the bite of the harness, the danger of the glass floor, and the black bowling balls sent at her by jealous others to 'trap this outrageous nimble queen' whose daring is clearly a challenge, their attack deadly. So a 'penalty for her skill' is the everyday threat of the streets and tall buildings, walking the 'steel gauntlets of traffic', terrified in case the 'elaborate scaffold of the sky' falls on her. The poem deals with images of power and individuality, fears about identity, male control, the temporary success of female daring.

EXPERIMENTS WITH STYLE

Other poems show her trying out, adapting the language and forms of poets who have influenced her, such as Dylan Thomas and Emily Dickinson among others. She writes of death, of spring, of love, of children, the instability of the seemingly stable everyday, Cinderella, Bluebeard – myths that relate to women's dreams and roles. She also writes of possible roles for the creative woman. The writer in 'Female Author' resembles the late romantic fiction writer, Barbara Cartland, pictured in pink flounces and heavy doll-like makeup, she 'pink-breasted, feminine, nurses chocolate fancies in rose-papered rooms'. In danger of total retreat from the world, she is overtaken by images of romantic love: 'sick', 'crypt', 'festering', 'hothouse'.

The 'Juvenilia' establishes Plath's concerns, themes and images. They show how she starts to develop her own voice, working through different forms, setting up patterns and repetitions in and between the poems, dealing with contradictory images of woman, life, writing, love, death, identity.

The Colossus

In *The Colossus* (1960) Plath's interests in landscapes and settings, in death and in roles for women are established. Of the early poems (1956–1963), 'Ode for Ted' concentrates on her representations of the strong male, seeing the woman figure/ herself as 'this Adam's woman' – the mate, companion in the essential male–female relationship. The hunter is the role in which she cast Ted Hughes, seeing him as Adam and herself as Eve, his pursuits being the hunting down of animals; conquering and controlling. But she also works out her thoughts about myths and roles available to women, sometimes taking the persona of the woman who chooses celibacy or the woman whose sexuality is her identity.

Landscapes

Other poems look at her surroundings, her context, the place where she was brought up, such as 'Black Rock in Rainy Weather', 'Dream with Clam-Diggers', 'Mussel Hunter at Rock Harbour', 'Green Rock, Winthrop Bay' where she focuses on the landscape, with rocks. Upon moving to England she describes the scenes of Cambridge in 'Watercolour of Grantchester Meadows' and the North in 'The Snowman on the Moor'.

Other poems concentrate on the activities of people set against interior landscapes – the thought processes and worldviews of different personae whose worlds we visualise, even hearing the language they would use to describe their world and themselves. These interior landscapes are matched and balanced with those of her home or current surroundings. She explores ways of being, choices in 'The Beggars', 'Ella Mason and her Eleven Cats', 'Crystal Gazer'. It is dangerous to attribute to Plath herself all the views of the world, invented, visualised through the eyes of her persona. They could be aspects, versions of her seeing and being, but they are not all her own choices or actions directly transferred to a poem. However, some poems are more autobiographical than others. 'The Beekeeper's Daughter' references her father's bee keeping and her own balanced role between father and mother, establishing herself as a queen bee. Here is a queenship no mother can contest. In 'Wreath for a Bridal' Plath views her own wedding as a launching moment for union, harmony and a great ambitious future for them both.

Death

Not all the poems work through versions of seeing the world or deal fairly directly with her own experiences. Some provide discourses, discussions of lingering thoughts, worries and fears, concepts we all need to work through and some rather obsessional issues which linger in Plath's mind more than in the minds of readers. Death has great fascination for her, partly because of its finished quality, its completion, a kind of perfection in closure: which she equates with art. Offering peace and perfection, a culmination, death is seen as attractive and deadly together, seductive, a terrifying threat, something lurking, calling to her, letting her know that she can fail, tied up with success. In some of her poems there is a sense of surrender, the possibility of death, of 'not being', partly realised or embodied in terms of a horror of her work not being recognised, and partly as a personal loss of self and substance – both sought and feared. 'All the Dead Dears' looks closely at death and loss, in the archaeological sense, in Cambridge generations of families who 'reach hag hands to haul me in' as, immortalised in statues, lying on their tombs, they move through the ages, permanent, in stone. Throughout these poems which focus on the dead, Plath is wondering about the state of death and the state of living.

Birth and mothering

Several of Plath's poems concentrate on birth or mothering and of these poems 'You're'(1960) operates rather like a riddle. The poem is addressed to an unknown; 'you' who becomes a little clearer as the poem proceeds and more easily identifiable as the baby, before birth. The images are very unusual but appropriate for an unborn baby whose birth is awaited with great interest, eagerness and not a little apprehension. The child presents itself in the poem first of all as a clown, standing on its hands, which makes it sound jolly, lively, individualistic, but also refers to the birthing position of most babies, head down. Throughout the poem there are references to strangeness and newness: 'vague as fog and looked for like mail'; the baby is strange, its as yet not quite full human characteristics, its strangeness emphasised by comparing its skull to a moon. It has gills like a fish, it's a 'travelled prawn'. Other fishy images compare it to a 'sprat', a slippery 'creel of eels'. The child is strange as the fish images suggest – yet lively and alive, jumping, moving, moving on. Like a wholesome loaf it is a 'high riser'. This reflects its growth, its naturalness, the warmth the mother/ speaker feels towards this very natural, strange, awaited child. And strangeness continues with comparisons to a turnip, root crop, hardly seen until dug up. Comparison with the extinct bird, the dodo, celebrates success over death: this child's birth represents continuity, a 'thumbs down' or belying of the 'dodo's mode', extinction. The baby's shape is reflected in the images used – 'prawn', 'like a spool', the god atlas with a world on his back (the child wrapped up in the womb). Its movements within its mother are surprising, jumpy, then:

> Right, like a well-done sum.
> A clean slate, with your own face on.

> ('You're', p. 141)

This child is perfect, like a piece of maths properly completed and with many possibilities for development, fresh in life. The poem is realistic, amusing, childlike, and uses strange images: fish, the dodo, mail, to suggest what is both familiar and very strange to us, in this new baby. Plath carefully uses internal rhyme. Word sounds relate by comparison, contrast or building up a pattern. The internal rhyme causes us to relate word meanings, so in the first stanza 'skulled', 'gilled', 'spool', 'trawl', all echo each other, the changing vowels altering the sound while the 'l' repeats, linking the words. In the second stanza 'snug', 'bud', 'jug', 'sum', echo, linking the natural – bud – with the cosiness and care 'snug' and the perfect 'well done sum'.

Plath uses common place idioms, 'a clean slate' as well as unusual images, so making the familiar unfamiliar, new, fresh to us. Linking sounds together she unites strange images in the everyday, all contributing to this new way of seeing. These reflect the newness of an unborn child and the fresh surprise for its parents, who cannot fully imagine either what the child will be like/look like, or how their relationship with it will develop. This celebratory and lively poem is unusual: few such positive and honest poems are written to an unborn child. If the poem seems indecipherable, one of the main clues is in the nine month span between the Fourth of July, its original conception date, and All Fools' Day when it is born, arriving as a surprise.

Bee keeping

Plath's six bee-keeping poems were developed partly from her experience with keeping bees in childhood and again in adulthood. But more important, they act as a metaphor for the poet and the self. David Holbrook argued that someone so unsure of her own identity and lacking in the security and stability of self had a problem with 'be(e)ing' reflected in her bee-keeping poetry. The central image of the all powerful queen bee who is paradoxically kept a prisoner of her own creativity, at the centre of the hive, is one that makes us think of the mother, the captive housewife, the powerful poet. Plath's bee-keeping poems become a quest for a self and also a discourse upon power, being either authoritarian or democratic. In the first, as 'the Beekeeper's Daughter' she questions:

> ... but I
> Have a self to recover, a queen.
> Is she dead, is she sleeping?
> Where has she been ... ?

('Stings', p.215)

Mating with the queen bee in her nuptial flight is fatal for the drone she chooses. His abdomen splits upon the mating act. In 'The Bee Meeting' the initiation of a naive young girl's speaker parallels that of the removal of virgin bees, leaving the old queen to make a new hive. Old established figures, the sexton, midwife and rector watch with approval, their square black heads suggesting bees, gravity, ritual and death. She is a sacrificial victim in this, at the core of a secret. At the centre of the glade is a long white box and at the end of the poem the old queen and the girls are united in potential death.

Plath kept bees.

'The Arrival of the Bee Box' figures a horde of amicable bees kept
contained in a box and bursting to escape, but managed by the speaker
once she has gained control. She is fooling herself it seems, as the poem
progresses, for each assertion of control reveals the increased noise and
the fascination of the box of bees. She has here more than she can
handle and control is a con:

> I have simply ordered a box of maniacs.
> They can be sent back.
> They can die, I need feed them nothing, I am the owner.
>
> ('The Arrival of the Bee Box, p.213)

Bragging about controlling the uncontrollable follows in 'Stings',
'Wintering' and 'The Swarm', each dealing with issues of identity,
power. The contrast between powerful control and passivity is a
struggle, indicating construction of self and the writer's role: a process
of constructing meaning.

'Daddy'

One of her greatest and certainly her best known poems is the
controversial 'Daddy'. The poem has a huge aural effect in as much as
when we listen to it, it becomes haunting, repetitive, overwhelming just
as the memory of her father has haunted and overwhelmed her.
'Daddy', a friendly, close, childish term is controversial in the poem
because of the very abrasive, harsh way in which the speaker pictures
her father. This is partly the poem of a woman who reveals the
contradictory love/hate responses of her adolescence. It is a poem
exploring this love. But poets often speak in extremes to us, articulating
the hidden. We recognise our probably slightly less extreme selves
through their expression.

'Daddy' is also a poem very specifically related to Plath's own life. While
it speaks to our feelings about our fathers, particularly women's
feelings, it is also very peculiarly her own obsessional response to the
haunting of her life as a woman by the father who died in her

childhood. The poem is also literally a haunting, of both her father's memory and loss and it *sounds* like a haunting, with the repetitive 'oo' sound.

She begins with a rejection. Like a familiar old black shoe, her father (or rather her memory and image of him) is no longer appropriate, out of date. She seems to be trying to exorcise a dominant, intrusive image and influence by calling out his name:

Daddy, I have had to kill you.

('Daddy', p.222)

Use of concentration camp images

This is her first statement of exorcism and it is shockingly direct. But we then realise that he is already dead. Here Plath begins to grow the image of her father, his head as big as an seagoing seal, his importance emphasised by references to God and heaviness; 'a bag full of God'. He becomes a rock or sculpture, solid, over which everything else washes and flows. In establishing an image she can hold for herself, the narrator utilises a range of images of oppression. Plath has been criticised for using images and language referring to the Holocaust, but in so doing she is equating the horrors of personal suffering with human suffering and cruelty on a wider scale, relating the individual to history, using the historical to describe feelings. Unable to speak to him because he is dead/ over important, she feels like a Jewish victim in a Nazi concentration camp. That she cannot find the words to express her sense of love, loss and hatred is emphasised in equating this enforced silence with being snared by barbed wire:

The tongue stuck in my jaw.

It stuck in a barb wire snare.
Ich, ich, ich, ich,

('Daddy', p.223)

His order and brutality, expressed in stereotypical and mythic images of the Nazi, is contrasted to her vulnerability and mystery, her alternative ways with a tarot pack to feel the future through supernatural, alternative powers. The diatribe against her father builds up momentum until she equates Fascism with relationships, emphasising the compelling sado-masochistic relationship she has with this memory but also asserting that women like and need strong men: an assertion which has come in for a great deal of feminist criticism.

It can indeed be related back to the poems Plath wrote on meeting Ted Hughes, being her imagining of the ideal and desire for a strong man, strong enough to be her equal or teacher. It is also an image of the indescribable contact she has with her father after death, which emerges in terms such as 'the black telephone's off at the root'. Further, it is the culmination of a developing theme about the oppressive memory, the love–hate relationships of which she is aware, of which she knows she must attempt to escape if she is to become an adult. In her visual memory the oppression of her father emerges in Nazi, death imagery.

Standing at the blackboard in her memory, as he does in one of the few remaining pictures of him her father reminds her of a devil with a cleft his foot. She equates him with a lover, a man who has stolen her heart, who 'bit my pretty red heart in two'.

Images of oppression and dominance develop into horror images. He is a vampire, a creature from a tomb or grave whose power cannot be avoided even after death. The gothic horror imagery builds up – he is 'a man in black with a **Mein Kampf** look' (a reference to Hitler) and a love of torture.

KEYWORD

Mein Kampf: This was Hitler's polemical work which set out his intentions to conquer the world.

She cannot avoid his contact even though she insists she now rejects it, emphasised through the image of the black, grave telephone whose 'voices just can worm through'. It is severed, ripped up at the root, yet by insisting that it has no effect and cannot be heard, Plath is, in fact, letting it be heard. She tries to exorcise her father. The whole folktale community help her, dancing round his grave, staking him, vampire-like at the crossroads. Nonetheless the strength of her father's oppressive memory is greater than her insistence on his exorcism. The haunting 'oo' sound throughout the poem, rhyming with 'you' makes the address to her father constant, his reference throughout inescapable. She might have found out the culprit, 'They always knew it was you' insisting she and her father, as if a couple, are now split apart. 'Daddy, daddy you bastard, I'm through', but the protestations suggest he will return in her mind (as in all good horror scenarios).

The language is colloquial, conversational, immediate. 'I'm through', ' you bastard'. Internal and end rhyme is repetitive and insistent. An example of the ways in which the internal rhyme emphasises the senses is 'stuck', 'ich', 'speak'. She is snared and silenced, forced to speak his language, the German 'ich'. Although the end rhyme is repetitive and dominant, it does not overwhelm but enables the sense and mood to be developed. The lines run on, using **enjambement** rather than being **end-stopped**. The whole is overwhelming, enveloping, insistent.

KEYWORDS

Enjambement: a poetry term referring to lines in poetry where the sense runs on from one line to the next.

End-stopped: where the sense of a line of poetry is completed at the end of the line.

Death and renewal

In 'Daddy' Plath refers to her suicide attempts and in 'Lady Lazarus' she works through her (ultimately tragic) arguments about rising anew from death, renewing life. 'Lady Lazarus' is a powerful, dominant poem with an insistent rhythm and rhyme, much like 'Daddy', this time celebrating the speaker's power to defy death and cast off oppressive

relationships with men and life. Recalling the earlier 'Aerialist' the colloquial, conversational voice is that of a performer celebrating and showing off, relating to a rapt audience her greatest daring acts and showing her scars of earlier suicide attempts. Use of the first person 'I' throughout emphasises the showmanship. Her tone is that of the trickster at a sideshow, calling us in as spectators to marvel.

We become part of the 'peanut crunching crowd;' pushing in to see her being unwrapped, released from a mummified state, restored to life, the worms picked off her. The worms stand for the grave and also as they are pearls, to Shakespeare's *The Tempest* where Ferdinand, the King's son is said to have his eyes turned to pearls as he lies with the fishes. He is restored to life, as she claims to be. In the Bible, Lazarus was raised from the dead by Christ. What the speaker insists on is a miracle in a sideshow, calling on us to be her witnesses as Plath rehearses a suicide attempt every decade and pulls through:

I am only thirty.
And like the cat I have nine times to die.

('Lady Lazarus', p.244)

The tone of celebration and showmanship builds up.

Plath invites us as voyeurs into her own life/death scenario; we are audience and judge. The charge we pay to see bits of her on show, a ghoulish celebration of her death defying act, is also an electric charge, a bolt, revitalising her. As in 'Daddy', Plath uses Nazi oppression imagery addressing 'Herr Doctor' as her enemy, the figure of death. She refers to the burning up of millions of Jews in concentration camps, the remains only gold rings and teeth fillings. From such oppressive destruction, she insists on her own phoenix-like rising, a daring, harpy figure who challenges men.

'Edge' is probably Plath's last poem. The static, sculpted aesthetic beauty embodies a mythical sacrificial role for the dead woman. Performative, self-aware, Plath's personae dare and celebrate death, to outlast it, as if it were 'an art'. But in reading these poems which so dangerously align life/death and art we need to be conscious of the technical artistry of the language – internal rhyme, connected images, references to interpretations of myths, adopted sounds and voices. This is a superb performance whether she writes of death and art, self and identity or motherhood. Plath's images came to life and she captures the sounds and images of the everyday world of myth, of the sensitivities of the inner self. Her poetry often works on patterns of sound and image rather than straightforward translatable storyline. She writes for the ear, the aesthetic.

✳ ✳ ✳ ✳SUMMARY ✳ ✳ ✳ ✳

- Sylvia Plath's major poems deal with the contradictions of her age and women's roles.

- Her works are individually structured, rich in pattern and images and her works as a *whole* shows recurring interests and developing techniques.

6 Major works: the prose

THE BELL JAR (1963)

Semi-fictionalised biography

The Bell Jar is Plath's best known creative prose work and is a major contribution to the developing genre of women's writing which explores the self, personal history and identity through the semi-fictionalised autobiographical form. Bessie Head's *A Question of Power* (1974) is another example as is Maya Angelou's personal chronicle, which begins with *I Know Why the Caged Bird Sings*.

Being stifled

The semi-fictional form provides an opportunity for Plath to work out her past through her writing, turning it into a creative work as she articulates and shapes it. *The Bell Jar* itself is named after the airless jar that covers something and preserves it, perhaps also stifling it in the process. Esther in *The Bell Jar*, protected and preserved, is also in danger of suffocating, closed in by all the versions of self and identity which appear to her on the threshold of adulthood. Plath balances the protagonist's desire to be a successful writer and editor and a wife. Esther wins a magazine prize and summer editorial role, as did Plath (for *Mademoiselle*). These sit alongside a certain sexual angst and fear of sexual activity, of pregnancy and maternity. Like Plath she seeks solace and peace in the artistry of death as escape. When she recovers it is as if she has been buried. It is tempting to read *The Bell Jar* as an elaborated diary.

Life into art

This would not be a fair acknowledgement of the ways in which Plath has developed and transmuted her personal experiences into art, articulating and forming them into something more complex and also more accessible and generalisable than a personal record would be.

However, in terms of biographical critical reading, it is a rich source for a study of how a writer does indeed turn life into art. Along with the journals, *The Bell Jar* provides many clues about the contradictions in Plath's own thoughts and her developing sense of self. There are many echoes of the themes and concerns from the poems in the language used in the novel.

Chinese boxes

The process of reading *The Bell Jar* is less terse: it is more easily accessible than the highly wrought, tightly constructed compact poems. It presents us with a narrative we can piece together, although time does not run chronologically throughout the book. And it presents us with a central protagonist, Esther Greenwood, whose thoughts and life we follow. The shape of the novel has been compared to a series of Chinese boxes rather than a linear progression. This is a novel about breakdown and breakthrough, the creative, imaginative young woman sorting out her feelings about love, sex, her identity, her

Esther begins her breakdown and recovery.

role as a woman and as a creative writer. It speaks to all of us because it is about personal development, but it is not merely self conscious and inward looking. *The Bell Jar* is a rite of passage novel. Esther experiences a great deal, reflects on this and changes and develops accordingly. It is a novel with a historical context, in that it fits in with Plath's work as whole. Her poems use personal imagery and in the most intensely self-absorbed, complexly symbolic poems, she often takes contemporary images and uses these images and references to express her own arguments and the pain of the personal. Hers is very imaginative, self-absorbed, symbolic writing, which is also historically referenced.

Laying ghosts

Plath's mother and editor, Aurelia Plath, appended a letter to *The Bell Jar* (1970) saying that because Sylvia was laying so many ghosts in her novel, she did *not* want it to be published, (it came out in the UK in 1963, and in the USA in 1971). Aurelia Plath argued that Sylvia Plath had seen *The Bell Jar* as a 'potboiler; thrown together different parts from my own life, fictionalising to add colour' and that it aimed to show 'how isolated a person feels when he is suffering a breakdown … to picture my world and the people in it as seen through the distorted lens of a bell-jar'.

The search for identity

The Bell Jar begins with the summer of the Rosenberg trial and execution, felt along Esther's nerves – a lingering horror and Esther's spell in New York City on the editorial staff of *Mademoiselle* magazine. Summer in the city for the country girl is dreary, flat. The narrative then moves backwards in time and inwards into her thoughts, revealing past incidents which link to her current anxieties, helping her to clarify her own sense of direction. There are a series of self-contained incidents which reference others, setting up a kind of dialogue – different ways of interpreting events, different moments which cast light on others. Here we see Esther, a young woman entering maturity, deciding between versions of what it means to be a woman. All of the women in the novel offer alternatives to her and she measures herself off against what they represent.

Her friends, Doreen and Betsy, represent good and bad girls: conventional representations of how women 'should' behave. Doreen is sophisticated and sexually attractive, bored and critical of conformity, a worldly-wise, rather decadent figure. She is a sharp contrast to Betsy, a stereotypical co-ed from Kansas who wants to settle down on a farm with a big family. One is maternal and matronly (and becomes a hospital matron) and the other a dangerous vamp. Esther tries to establish her identity between these opposites. She is bored with socially conformist success and equally unable to throw herself into a more deviant set of behaviours:

> I wondered why I couldn't go the whole way doing what I should any more. Then I wondered why I couldn't go the whole way doing what I shouldn't.

Her talents are doubted, her growing up into a sexual adult rather disgusting, lacking in fanfares and joy. When Buddy Willard, the boyfriend from back home, disgusts her by showing her his body, she comments that 'the only thing I could think of was turkey neck and turkey gizzards and I felt very depressed'. A disgust of the body and the runs into a description of childbirth where the woman lies with her feet in metal stirrups on an 'awful torture table'. She seems 'to have nothing but an enormous spider fat stomach and two little ugly spindly legs roped in the high stirrups'. While the baby was being born she never stopped making this 'unhuman wooing noise' and yet 'all the time, in some secret part of her mind that long, blind, doorless and windowless corridor of pain was waiting, to open up and shut her in again'. Esther's first sexual exploit with Irwin, is fast and produces massive haemorrhaging, from which she escapes to write, having entered into adulthood: 'I smiled in the dark. I felt part of a great tradition.'

Cadavers

One of the most gruesome moments in the novel is when Esther's medical student boyfriend, Buddy Willard, takes her to see the cadaver room. The bottles of foetuses in pickling fluid are an image permanently established in her mind (and that of the reader!) as we have already seen in 'Stillborn'.

This last baby seems to single Esther out and implicate her in the horror of dead pickled babies. Much of *The Bell Jar* deals with Esther's own sexual awakening and her surprise and disgust. Partly this is a young adult's response to the new and partly a fear that babies and marriages will themselves be imperfect and prevent writing – the creativity of the two activities could be at odds.

Mason Harris (*The Bell Jar, West Coast Review*, October, 1973, p.54–6) identified the novel as a piece of 'catharsis following a private sickness' but nevertheless, it evokes an age:

> Never, nowhere have I found so forceful a depiction of what it was like to be an adolescent in the stifling, hermetically – sealed world of the Eisenhower Fifties. The distorted sense of madness gives an authentic vision of a period which exalted the most oppressive zeal of reason and stability.

Margaret Shook, writing of *The Bell Jar* in a Smith College context, recognises two voices, the one like J.D Salinger, the other like the existentialist Albert Camus. In the first, a satirical portrait of the life and times of Smith College students in the fifties is very recognisable. In some parts of *The Bell Jar*, Plath's voice, as Esther the narrator, resembles a self aware undergraduate's satirising the oppressive limitations of her life as a young woman and scholar in days when the two were not felt to mix together. Although Esther is well aware of her talents and ambitions when speaking to editor Jay Cee, she is equally aware of the expectations of her times, that intellectual successes become secondary to marriage.

The domestic paradigm

However, Esther is also a product of the 1950s' insistence that women turn into housewives, a stereotype expressed in popular musicals such as 'Oklahoma', 'Guys and Dolls' and the films of Doris Day, in *Bobby Soxer* and cheerleader images. The lyrics of fifties' popular songs all resonate with the dreams of the girl next door and domestic bliss.

Esther, a talented academic is caught in the dating trap – expected to fit in with the demands of different young men, none of whom is appealing to her, attracted towards yet rather horrified by the constraints of marriage, motherhood and a domestic life in which the husband has the last word.

Esther later says she should learn shorthand and typing since the academic life was not going to help her be a good wife or to earn a living. Shook talks of a 'half-humorous, half-stoical acceptance' of the contradictory lives these bright girls felt were waiting for them. Plath indicates conflicts when Esther says: 'I will be flying back and forth between one mutually exclusive thing and another for the rest of my days' (p.104)

Satirically aware comments align with other voices of her day offering comparisons for many striving for creative/ academic success yet aware of the pressures and promises of domestic life.

Existentialism

Esther speaks not only for her own generation but to other generations too. Critics generally do not have many problems with this element of *The Bell Jar* but when it turns into a narrative about dissociation of body from mind, **existentialism** and breakdown, there are more difficulties. One such passage illustrates this: Esther sees a shoe:

> It was a stout shoe of cracked black leather and quite old, with tiny air holes in a scalloped pattern over the toe and a dull polish and it was pointed at me. It seemed to be placed on a grass green surface and that was hurting my right cheekbone.

I kept very still, waiting for a clue that would give me some notion of what to do, a little to the left of the shoe I saw a vague heap of blue cornflowers on a white ground and this made me want to cry. It was the sleeve of my own bathrobe I was looking at, and my left hand lay pale as a cod at the end of it.

(*The Bell Jar*, p.149)

Initially she cannot recognise the shoe or robe and feels dissociated from them.

KEY FACT

Existentialim:

Existentialism probably originated in France in the 1940s. It is a belief system that states:

1 There are no ultimate rules, rewards or meanings. The idea of a God is also refuted. So all our actions are both entirely *and* ultimately 'absurd' (that is, lacking in a regimented and fixed meaning within a system of meaning of life).
2 People label the world, make meaning, through words but actually, every experience is new, strange and we try to make it familiar and safe through these word labels.
3 Without fixed systems, roles, laws, meanings the individual can only strive fully to experience their own sense of existing or being in the world, as themselves living and experiencing. Jean Paul Sartre and Albert Camus, French philosophers, both wrote from an existentialist point of view. One response to existentialism could be to feel in despair – nihilism – nothing has point or value or meaning. Another is to feel freedom, to construct reasons, the self, beliefs, *knowing* it is all a construction and existence and the world in unity does *not* have meaning, beliefs, rewards or punishments – *we* place these over existence and the world.

Sartre's narrator in *Nausea* feels the door handle is something quite other and disgusting and cannot label it when he takes it to open the door. Esther also feels disgust at existence, at matter, and her own body when she recognises the hand lying out of the bathrobe as her own and so expresses it as a dead fish, a cod – other, cold, lumpen.

Existential insights show a macabre interest in death. Esther attempts suicide and undergoes shock treatment.

JOHNNY PANIC AND THE BIBLE OF DREAMS (1977)

Although Plath wrote approximately 70 short stories, only ten were published in her lifetime. Seven appear in *Johnny Panic*, a collection of stories, prose and diary excerpts which marked the first release of any parts of Plath's diaries/ journals, the bulk of the remainder of which were recorded and published in 2000.

She writes in one autobiographical piece: 'I sometimes think my vision of the sea is the clearest thing I own' (Ocean 1212-W). 'In Context', a five paragraph comment on her poetry published in the *London Magazine*, is where she notes her influences and her work: 'The poets I delight in are possessed by their poems as by the rhythms of their own breathing', which says much about her own closeness to her poetry and the developing of a speaking voice relying on breathing rather than end rhymes.

Some poetic excerpts are put in the story section of the book because of the elaborations on real events so 'Fifteen Dollar Eagle' describes a sailor being tattooed – painfully and bloodily and 'Mothers' describes a Devon mothers' union tea meeting.

In the short stories, the plots are not complex and much of the writing is more like pieces produced to order, within tight structural rules ready for presentation in class rather than imaginative, original insightful work. But we do see here similar images and interests which emerge in the poems. In 'Sunday at the Mintons'(1952) a brother and sister, the one rational, preoccupied with clocks, the other a lavender-loving spinster, live in a mutually destructive dreamlike world: 'Hers was a twilight world, where the moon floated up over the trees at night like a tremulous balloon of silver light.' Plath's fears of the life of the spinster emerge here, as can be seen in the contrived ending where both die in a dreamy, watery way.

Another death ends 'The Wishing Box' (1957), which focuses on a couple, Agnes and Henry. He mingles with the rich and famous but she is empty of images, in a domestic prison, her mind empty of anything that does not coincide with her world and life. Her suicide provides a tableau of self-fulfilment, performativity and revenge – she lies with an open pill box, on the sofa. In her mind, she is waltzing with an ideal prince of her early dreams: 'On the sofa … dressed in her favourite princess-style emerald taffeta evening gown pale and lovely as a blown lily … [she had a] secret smile of triumph, as if, in some far country unattainable to mortal men, she was there, at last, waltzing with the dark, red-caped prince of her early dreams.'

Artistic characters

Many of Plath's characters in the short stories are either artistic or intent upon creating versions of themselves in artwork. Several, perceiving a split between the inner self and the outer world, tend to breakdown, or commit suicide. Much of this fiction is seen as working through themes later developed in *The Bell Jar*. In 'Stone Boy with Dolphins', Dody Ventura longs for something to happen in the depth of her own dreams, filled with visionaries such as Joan of Arc.

It is gothic and nightmarish, aims to emphasise the split between the self in the imagination and the shared external world which is seen as safe but dull. The narrator of the title piece, *Johnny Panic and the Bible of Dreams*, however, is well aware of a split between the world of the imagination and fantasy and that of the 'real', shared world, which can be experienced as a hard, cold world ordered in a limiting fashion. This story takes up a theme and an insight more commonly seen in the 1960s and 1970s, that the shared world is itself a construction, something we impose upon a hard cold 'outside' ourselves. In this world we each use our imagination to create the world in a different and unique way.

LETTERS HOME (1975)

'The joy of being a loved and loving women: that is my song.' (1956)

Letters Home was edited by Plath's mother, Aurelia Plath, in 1975, probably partly to set the story straight about their relationship which had undergone rather unpleasant metamorphosis into the artistic version of a relationship between Esther Greenwood and her own mother in *The Bell Jar*. It provides insights into the developing mind of a strong-willed, creative young woman, well aware of the roles society demands of her. Plath is shown to be prone to extreme mood swings and to be in love with life to the full.

We can see instead someone in love with her youth: 'Now, now is the perfect time of my life' (on being 17); 'I have never before had so much together' and in love with Ted Hughes: 'I met the strongest man in the world … a singer, story-teller, lion and world-wanderer … this man, this poet, this Ted Hughes.'

In this collection we are not aware of the suicidal part of the writer. She intends to be both a strong woman aware of her own ability and equality and achievement and a wife and mother to have it both ways:

> I shall be one of the few women poets in the world who is fully a rejoicing women not a bitter or frustrated or warned man-imitator, which ruins most of them in the end, I am a woman and glad of it and my songs will be of fertility and of the earth.

She is also seen as a rejoicing mother saying of the birth of their first child, Frieda: 'Our life seems to have broadened and deepened wonderfully with her'. But there are many absences from the last months of her life when she was writing the *Ariel* poems and especially after the visit of her mother. Some critics (Anne Tyler, *National Observer*, January 10 1976, p.19) find a chatty outer self, a performance in *Letters Home*, some others see a bright insincerity, the tone of a letter writer creating a sense of everything going smoothly. Others including Erica Jong see the variety of this volatile and talented woman artist, with the angry letters towards the end and notice the gaps in letters never written or never published.

JOURNALS (1982 AND 2000)

The publication of Plath's journals caused a stir and enabled critics to revalue the years with Ted Hughes as well as some of her last months. Pulling together parts of the jigsaw puzzle of her life is more possible now that later love entries have been restored. Plath 's women friends emerge as supportive, caring, but clearly also unable to help her stabilise in the last months. We have a view into a woman writing at the peak of creativity, using friends, depressed, pleased with her poetry, often very unhappy, often rather dissociated from reality. If the journals help us to fit some of the puzzle together, perhaps we can turn from the life to Plath's great art again and focus on its great creative wealth, rather than hints towards a suicide.

✳✳✳✳SUMMARY ✳✳✳✳

- Plath's prose and poetry deal with similar themes, use patterns and repetition, adapt imaginary worlds, personae, voices.

- She inhabits both the real and the imagined world.

- The main motifs are the self, the woman and the artist.

Contemporary criticism

7

Sylvia Plath's work was published in magazines and journals during her life. Her first book *The Colossus and Other Poems* appeared in 1960 and her novel *The Bell Jar* initially under the pseudonym 'Victoria Lucas' on January 14 1963. Other books, most notably the *Ariel* poems, written largely in 1962 and 1963, appeared after her death and her *Collected Poems*, edited by her husband, Ted Hughes were published in 1981.

POSITIVE REACTION

Early opinion of Plath's work was divided but mainly positive. The early critics found in her poetry a sure, highly educated, intelligent voice matched with careful control of language and form. American reviewers found her more derivative. Dickey, Whittemore and Myers said her tone was narrow in range, her poetry impersonal but promising.

Commentary which appeared during her life largely welcomed her work, but the moment of her death on February 11 1963 changed the tone and the bulk of critics began to read her work through her life or rather through her death, directing all the work until that point as if aimed at that death, finding it excessive, taut and unbalanced. Questions about the relationship between her life and art dominated criticism with many worrying that she had elided the two fatally, others arguing that the creative process tied to the emotional process, when explored to its limit by a woman writer, produced such imbalances as were fatal. She then became the focus of both autobiographical and rather conservative criticism.

OUTSTANDING TECHNICAL ACCOMPLISHMENT

The early positive reviews seem largely forgotten but are worth considering in gaining a more balanced sense of her work as a whole.

'A real find, exhilarating to read' commented Peter Dickinson on 'The Colossus', in *Punch* 1960, noting that Plath's ambiguities differentiated from the abstractions of American poets in general and focused on concrete experience with 'clean, easy verse'. Bernard Bergonzi (*Manchester Guardian Review* no. 6) recognised influences from John Crowe Ranson and Theodore Roethke but insisted on Plath's as an original voice with 'virtuous' qualities and 'outstanding technical accomplishment' unlike, he argues, the general writing by women of the day. He says she 'writes of people or natural objects in a detached yet sympathetic way, with a fastidious vocabulary and a delicate feeling for the placing of the individual word'.

Alvarez also finds her work 'bare but vivid and precise in language', 'tense and twisted … ominous, odd' comparing her work to Grimm's fairytales and the language of contemporary women's writing in general. Other poets and critics, such as John Wain and Roy Fuller, thought her power brilliant, her half-rhymes and organisation perfectly controlled with a deep consciousness of the physical world. Alvarez found her work clever, 'vivacious', individual, although he also saw it as mysterious and her avoidance of direct expression hid, he argued 'a sense of threat, as though she were certainly menaced by something she could only see out of the corner of her eyes' (*Observer*, December 18 1960).

A.E. Dyson (*Critical Quarterly*, summer, 1961 pp.181–5) sees a 'lurking menace' beneath much of what she describes or evokes, arguing that she prefers landscapes that suggest wildness and threat rather than the tamed alternatives and that she feels an affinity with death. Dyson characterises her poetry as distinct from that of Ted Hughes. Plath is 'brooding and tentative'. One is more clearly powerful, the other more 'intermingled with hallucination and conjecture', ironic, yet affected by a world suffused with what Dyson identifies as a kind of religious power.

SUICIDAL INFLUENCES
Beginning a discussion to her work, Charles Newman (*The Art of Sylvia Plath*, 1971) concentrates on two critical versions, the first seeing her

poems as *strikingly* autobiographical, the second as merely fashionable because filled with hints of the suicidal and with existential angst. *Both* versions connect her to the roles of shrill, mad suicide and concentrate on the last poems. Initially, one of the most voiced critical appraisals was that of A. Alvarez, the journalist and critic who visited her before her death and defined her in *The Savage God* (1971) as a great writer shadowed by oncoming suicide. When Plath died Alvarez wrote in *The Observer*: 'The loss to literature is inestimable.'

The linking of her poetry and her suicide has stamped her indelibly on readers' minds as one whose work can be seen as hints and patterns leading towards that suicide. 'The achievement of her internal style is to make poetry and death inseparable', wrote Alvarez, recognising the danger. 'Poetry of this order is a murderous art.'

Plath was only 31 when she died and such a young death casts her in the same mould as other young deaths or suicides, writers whose great talents have been cut short. This includes John Keats, the Romantic poet, who also died young over a century earlier (of tuberculosis). It relates her to the Romantic Chatterton who committed suicide after his forged poems were discovered and to Virginia Woolf, the great **Modernist** author who had bouts of depression and drowned herself, depressed by the Second World War. It also relates her closely to Robert Lowell and Anne Sexton, her friends and influences, both of who committed suicide. Robert Lowell, who taught the writing class Sexton and Plath attended, established a view of her as a great, tragic heroine, a genius, a woman of extremes who writes her best when suffering these extremes:

> **KEYWORD**
>
> Modernism: a term used to describe the literary movement of the 1890s–1940s whose international writers numbered among them T.S Eliot, Virginia Woolf, James Joyce and Ezra Pound. They wanted to write in a new way, rejecting the tired conventions of the nineteenth century and wished to 'make it new'. Complex technically, they often concentrated on disillusionment, fragmentation and a search for something to believe in.

> In these poems, written in the last months of her life and often rushed
> out at the rate of two or three a day, Sylvia Plath becomes herself,
> becomes something imaginary, newly, wildly, and subtly created (hardly
> a person at all, or a woman, certainly not another 'poetess', but one of
> those super-real, hypnotic, great classical heroines.
>
> (Marsack, 1992, p.11)

This view establishes her greatness, but labels her as superhuman, fated
because of her tragedy of being a creative female, rather like an ancient
prophetess, sacrificed somehow for her art. To some extent, several of
the early feminist critics who began to write on Plath in the early 1790s
took up this version of her. These critics however, turned it around,
seeing her death as a tragic consequence of the fatal contradictions
under which women live and were exacerbated in Plath's case because
of her hypersensitivity and poetic talent. This reads her as a symptom
of gender discrimination. It rewrites the hysteric as a woman seeking
sexual liberation, at a period when she had neither space nor place.

Others concentrate more on her technique and did not just see the
suicide lurking behind it. Ian Hamilton, also a poet (*London Magazine*,
July 1963, p.54–7) finds her first book sophisticated, her work in
danger of being controlled by her strange perceptions into a 'high class
game'. Instead the poetry can aid the expression of the control of
experiences. This is an important issue in Plath's work.

We should not see hers as a cry of pain, cry for help or a personal
outpouring but as a personal perception of life and the world carefully
controlled through expert techniques, through the poetry. Ian
Hamilton finds a 'minimum of personal involvement' in much of
Plath's poetry. Reading poetry through to the life would be a mistake.
Some argue she tried to write about the unbearable and in so doing her
art came too fatally close to her *life*.

EARLY REACTIONS TO *THE BELL JAR*

The Bell Jar, published just before Plath died, also received a variety of attention with critics pointing out how Plath (or Victoria Lucas – her pseudonym) was able to write in a personal yet detached way:

> It read so much like the truth that it is hard to disassociate her from Esther Greenwood, the 'I' of the story, but she had the gift of being able to feel and yet to watch herself: she can feel the desolation and yet relate it to the landscape of everyday life.
>
> (anonymous review, *TLS*, January 25 1963, p.53)

Laurence Lerner (*Listener* January 31 1963, p.215) equates this detachment with Esther's neurosis deriving from her role as satirist of the world around her. Esther has a personal 'bell jar', which descended on her even before she won the competition and worked as a guest editor in New York for a summer. Lerner notes readability and an 'almost poetic delicacy of perception'. Some of other students' and Plath's early work in college magazines resembles *The Bell Jar*. Esther's experiences are a parody of Plath's and the novel is a satirical one (dealing with college life's demands of creativity, dating, academic work, establishing identity.

ARIEL – ANOTHER LEVEL

Plath's greatest poetry collection is undoubtedly *Ariel*, which she wrote in the early mornings over a couple of years preceding her death. But her work should be viewed as a whole because there is such a tight link between themes and expression, as her voice develops and her techniques become her own. The collection repeats certain images and metaphors throughout – dealing with events in life, the family, writing, identity, death.

Alvarez sees her death (*Observer*, March 1 1965, p.20) as if produced by the poetry, 'like some final unwritten poem' which brings it all a little *too* close together. In his final analysis of the poems, Alvarez comments that while earlier poems were written for the eye – that is, technical, laid out in an acceptable form – the latter are written for the ear and they capture her own developed speaking voice, her own.

CONTRADICTIONS AND PARADOXES

Alvarez also points out her use of colloquial language, controlled, technically refined and perfected; the personal involvement and the detachment; the generosity in celebration of life; and the **nihilism**. There are contradictions, paradoxes in Plath's poetry: 'We would be very limited in our reading of her to settle for one version alone.' Rosenthal (*Spectator*, March 19 1965, p.367) sees her

> **KEYWORD**
>
> Nihilism: the belief that life is devoid of meaning, usually coupled with a denial of religious belief or moral principles. The predominant mode in literature in a sense of despair.

having 'confusion of terror' at death and a 'fascination by it', a 'disgusted yet heroic picture' of her dominant father in the poem 'Daddy', a mixture of a brave facing-up to the horrors of the age – Auschwitz and Hiroshima – and an over-identification with these horrors as if she were victim and killer at once.

Plath's involvement with world events, her identification with its pains, her internalisation of much of this sense of the power of nature, the presence of death, sit alongside her technical skill of transmuting these personal responses into the artwork. She is a poet of opposites joined, of ambiguities and dichotomies. Peter Dale (*Agenda*, summer 1966, p.49–55) comments of the *Ariel* poems that the most successful are those that combine the private and the artistically articulated: 'Those were her highly private fears, guilts, failures and urges are made objective in concentrated situations such as in the bee-keeping poems, or 'Tulips'.'

DEATH AND RE-EVALUATION

Her death led critics to see all her poetry as leading, with hysterical and fatal intent, to that end. This frequently undercut the value of the tightly knit poetry, seeing it as either traumatised outpouring, almost unreadable, or as an example that the individual becomes lost, the quality of the work ignored, when driven by such a need to express a sense of dissociation from normal everyday life. Tellingly, it is suggested that this is rather a female trait, something that happens to women who (it is hinted by some critics) are more likely to find the clash between creative artistry and life tips them over into hysterical poetry and death.

Stephen Spender (*New Republic*, 18 June 1966, **23**, p.25–6) claims the last thing she cares about is her readers or prizes. She is driven by 'a pure need of expression certified ... by death'. He is lucid in his identification of how Plath turns external objects into internal symbols or feelings, how she fuses love and hatred, seeing in 'Letter in November' this process in the description of trees 'the wall of old corpses', the fruit gold balls (recalling myth) 'in a thick grey death-soup/ their million/ Gold leaves metal and breathless'. Spender resents the refusal to keep nature outside the poet in its seasonal flow, the need here to internalise and use the natural as a palette to paint inner feelings. He recognises in Plath a visionary who, like Wilfred Owen aims to 'warn' us of horrors but he argues that she has so denaturalised and defamiliarised the world she describes that everything is horrific, everything 'a symptom of the same holocaust' arguing that this too is peculiarly female: 'With Sylvia Plath, her femininity is that her hysteria comes completely out of herself, and yet seems about all of us. And she has turned our horrors about our achievements into the same witches' brew.'

Hers are poems of the 'visionary', 'the prophet'. P.N. Furbank (*Listener*, March 11, 1965, p.379) sees her poetry as 'sick verse', a hysterical gaiety and bravado driving the need to express the 'non-me'. Not denying the horror, Hugh Kenner (*Triumph*, September 1966, pp.33–4) refuses allegations that the poetry is uncontrolled, lost. Plath, he says, 'counting her lines and governing her rhetoric' measured, the mad 'wild child' vision in controlled stanzas, of five or three lines, in internal rhyme. He finds her attraction for contemporary readership in a kind of spiritual fascination with death in an age of materialism, secularity in search for spiritual shortcuts and disgust with matter. Some critics lapsed into an excess bt seing her work only as 'symphony of death and dissolution' not aiming for an audience, a private cry of a schizophrenic who had learned to produce poetry.

Later reviews of *The Bell Jar* also focus on the suicide as a central point. C.B. Cox (*Critical Quarterly*, autumn 1966, p.195) and J.D. O'Hara (*Washington Post Book World*, April 11 1971, p.3) identify two narratives in Esther Greenwood's tale, one the 'cheerful, shallow, fast-moving account' of the barely disguised biography of Plath's spell as guest editor on *Mademoiselle*, economically written, with a nineteen-year-old's tone, recording moments of dates, sickness, work and fun. This then dissolves into the second section that concentrates on the madness, psychiatric treatment, and sees in this split that of Plath and of young America itself; a golden girl on the outside, mad beneath.

* * * *SUMMARY * * * *

• The critics of her day initially recognised Plath's technical brilliance, her control of language and her unique voice.

• The tone of criticism changed with her death and many critics concentrated on reading her death back into everything she wrote.

Modern criticism

8

FURTHER REAPPRAISAL

Critics in the last 20 or so years of the twentieth century started to recuperate her work. Some followed a feminist point of view and came to recognise Plath as one of the great confessional poets whose autobiography affects our reading of her writing. Others see her as political. Pamela Annas, Stan Smith and Alan Sinfield read her as a 'profoundly political poet' (Smith, 'Waist Deep in History: Sylvia Plath' in *Inviolable Voice: History and Twentieth Century Poetry*, Macmillan, 1982, p.219). A further group perpetuate the image of her as a hysterical suicide and linger over the reading of suspicions about her life and relationship with Ted Hughes, through everything she writes.

The myths and testimonies surrounding Plath's life and her poetic expression and the schisms between critics and friends who side with differing versions of events, confound and defer much genuine analytical criticism and celebration of her work. Stepping into this critical fray is dangerous, but necessary.

There are three main contemporary strands in criticism of Sylvia Plath's work: the **psycho-biographical**, the **cultural materialist** and the **feminist**.

THE PSYCHO-BIOGRAPHICAL

There is no problem with reading a poet's work through their life insofar as to some extent we all write from our experiences. However, to read the poetry as *only* a direct record of or comment upon a life would be a

KEYWORDS

Cultural materialism: the study of historical material within a politicised framework such as Marxism.

Feminism: the study of gender politics from a female perspective. Usually the term is applied to the political and social movement which swept Western Europe and the United Stated beginning int he late 1960s.

Psycho-biographical: in literature this is interpreting an artist's work as an index of their mental state and reading their menetal state as a way of interpreting the work.

mistake. Biographical criticism tends to foreground the biographical details and read the poetry through the biography or the biography through the poetry, seeing the one as an index of the other. In Plath's case this tends to lapse into speculations about how her whole body of work hints at unhappiness, leading up to the suicide. However, a more insightful biographical reading would look for fuller details on the one hand and more evidence of an artistic articulation on the other.

Psycho-biography unites the psychological with the biographical so that critics concentrate on elements of a writer's fears, fantasies, dreams. These critics speculate about a writer's psychological makeup, whether and in what way they are working out problems about their relationships with their family, their sense of identity, their sense of wholeness as a person.

Transmutation

Such criticism of Plath, tends to concentrate on the pathological, looking at issues such as breakdown, hysteria and schizophrenia. The focus is on Plath, the hysterical suicide. For example, they regard the poem 'In Plaster' as evidence of her schizoid state and all the poems dealing with death such as 'Death and Co.', 'All the Dead Dears', as prequels to the acting out of her final suicide. They are more properly the workings out of or explorations of relations between the inner subjective self and the shared world and (often rather **gothic**) musings and discussions about existence, self, time and death.

KEYWORD

Gothic: a term linked to gothic architecture and used to describe a stylised form which uses elements of the sinister and gro-tesque, usually to create claustrophobic settings and situations. Mary Shelley's Frankenstein is a gothic novel and includes all of the elements including old castles and a sense of darkness and danger, all wrapped up with a hint of roman-ticism.

Plath acknowledges the personal connection with the world, with the self as filter, saying: 'I think my poems immediately come out of the sensuous and emotional experiences I have but also that I believe that one should be able to control and manipulate experiences' (1962 interview with Peter Orr). She does not want to write about a 'kind of shut-box and internal-looking narcissistic experience'.

This is an acknowledgement that personal experience can fuel the material or poetry and a recognition that material is what it is, it is neither the whole substance nor the whole story. This material is transmuted by the artist. It would be insulting to her craft to suggest that the poems are only records of her life experiences – not least because it would be quite difficult in most cases directly to recognise specific experiences. They are, rather, emotional, reflective, speculative and creative responses to the world around her.

Much psycho-biographical criticism emerged immediately after Plath's death, but more has been produced in response to the gradual emergence of the *Letters Home* (1975) and the *Journals* (2000). Erica Jong (*L.A. Times Book Review*, November 23 1975, **1**, p.10) recognises the consciousness-raising and female rage of Plath's work overall and comments on the work: 'These were deeply felt perceptions of a consummate artist who had made a journey into her own personal hell and was bringing back the truth that only a voyager of genius into the nether regions of the communal unconscious can retrieve.' She argues 'the suicide theorists wanted something to theorise about' with Plath and seized on her, reading her death into all her work.

CULTURAL-MATERIAL AND HISTORICAL CRITICISM
Plath and the historical moment
Plath's opening sentences of *The Bell Jar* indicate her close identification with the brutal moment in history when Ethel and Julius Rosenburg were electrocuted for 'political' crimes. Lucas Myers comments on Plath's engagement with the historical moment – nuclear fallout, militarism, concentration camps and the trial of Nazi War criminal Adolf Eichmann. Stan Smith, **Marxist historicist** critic, points out Plath's self-identification with the historical moment. She is not merely an intensely private poet but one aware of the historical

connectedness of the self. He looks at 'Winter Trees' and 'Morning Song' arguing: 'It is precisely because her poetry is intensely private that it records so profoundly and distinctly the experience of living history. In Plath's poetry, there is no gap between private and public, (Smith, 'Waist-Deep in History: Sylvia Plath', p.202). She writes of herself in imagery, recalling the Holocaust ('Daddy') and in 'Lazy Lazarus', Japanese victims of nuclear war.

> **KEYWORDS**
>
> **Marxist historicism** a branch of cultural materialism which analyses texts using the ideas of Karl Marx.
>
> **Ideology:** a set of beliefs (ideas), systematised so that it applies to a class or individual, often as a basis of some economic or political theory or system.

Alan Sinfield's work (*Literature, Politics and Culture in Post-war Britain*, 1989) explores **ideological** intersections behind society and art, foregrounding Plath through whom those major contradictions are played. He criticises male critics for disempowering and stereotyping her and labelling hers a generalised psychotic disorder. Using a Marxist analysis of women's post-war cultural experience he recognises Plath as critiquing the construction of gender role arguments, taken up by some contemporary feminist critics.

FEMINIST CRITICISM

Another main strand of criticism on Plath which has largely recuperated and valued her voice as speaking for many other women is that of feminist criticism. Plath is seen to articulate many of the thoughts and feelings many women have about the constraints, opportunities and contradictions of women's social roles. As a great contemporary woman poet, Plath has scotched the image of the delicate, prissy poetess and gives us instead highly crafted, sensitive, powerful poetry. In this she has done much for establishing the power and value of women's poetry. Some feminist critics have, however instead sought in Plath a martyr to the sufferings of women in their subordinated social position.

L'écriture féminine

Feminist critics tend to concentrate on the representation of women in writing by both men and women; on women's writing; and on establishing a history of that writing; and on what is known as l'écriture féminine.

Writing the body

Feminist critics have established the notion of women 'writing the body'. This can be writing about the bodily experience of being a woman, a celebration, a specific recognition or it can be about the body in the world, expressing experience as a person in the senses and feelings. Plath has been recuperated by feminist critics of all castes since the late 1970s when feminist criticism really began to clarify this line of argument.

> **KEYWORD**
>
> L'écriture féminine: The belief that there is a particular kind or kinds of writing specific to women in terms of expression, imagery, tone, as well as subject matter and writing of 'the body'. This is a critical belief that women write through and of their bodies. The fact that they are also bodies in the world affects the way they see, feel, experience and also express themselves. This perception will be different from those of men.

Some of the elements of Plath's work that have been seized on by feminist critics concern her exploration of the different roles available to women.

Several feminist critics have noted how Plath negotiates her way through the stereotypes of spinster – ('Spinster') restricted, shrivelled, restrained, inviolate, perfect, the strumpet, flaunting her sexuality, attracting the interest and then the violence of all the men ('Strumpet Song') and the earth mother, wallowing in fecundity and childbirth, in childrearing, losing her mind and other forms of creativity ('Two Sisters of Persephone'). Plath debates constrained choices, explores extremes.

The Bell Jar and the body

Played out in a materialistic cultural context which seemed limited and shallow, *The Bell Jar* satirically details absurd, unpleasant, loveless, sexual encounters. It makes direct links between scientifically presented, distasteful sexual activity, the body and the inhuman sounding pains of childbirth. Birth and marriage are seen as experiences which could fulfil but also alienate you from yourself, from your own individuality. These are rather extreme versions of many young people's concerns about identity, individuality, the expectations of gender relations and entering the world of couples, social constraints, reproduction, settling down.

Feminist manifesto

Plath is not against love, sex, relationships with men; she is working through the myths and the realities, trying to find and express her own way of handling these contradictions. She explores the limitations on women, of women's achievements, and on relationships at *her own point in time*. Her desire to succeed in both the academic/ creative world *and that* of marriage is clearly articulated. Teresa de Lauretis (*Women's Studies*, 1976, pp.173–4) sees *The Bell Jar* as having attained the status of a 'feminist manifesto'.

She notes Plath's ability to integrate 'the historic **diachronic** self' (the heroine in her contemporary world) with a **synchronic**, timeless, mythical structure, the descent-ascent pattern, in which the heroine 'mediates the transition from one world to another or from one state of being to another'. Her story mixes guilt, loneliness, distaste at people behaving like automatons and mannequins, with tales of dating and near rape.

KEYWORDS

Diachronic: looking at the self or a work of art over a period of time, as a historic development.

Synchronic: looking at something as being closely attached to its time with no historic influences.

Rebirth and transfiguration are not quite achieved in the novel but are suggested as a third term in the birth, death and rebirth theme. De Lauretis finds Esther speaks to many women at different times, caught in cultural contradictions. Her potential for self-aware rebirth provides hope.

OTHER VIEWS

Plath was intent on motherhood and gained a great deal of happiness and satisfaction from her children whom she celebrates in a range of poems. Raymond Smith (*Modern Poetry Studies*, 1972, p.91–3) argues of Plath's dramatised poem, 'Three Women', 'the poem expresses with great sensitivity the wide range of feelings associated with this central factor of womanhood', that is childbirth. The comments of the three women all concentrate on childbirth: 'I cannot help smiling at what I know' from the pregnant one, 'there is this cessation', mourns the second after a miscarriage and 'there is a cessation of everything' from the third. Plath is sensitive about pregnancy and satirical, commenting on absent fathers and on the male ego, for example in the poem 'Gigolo'.

Humour in *Collected Poems*

A collected work always allows readers to move back and forth through the variety of the poetry and this helps establish continuities, as one might expect in a published career which at its height spanned only seven years. The inclusion of the pieces entitled 'Juvenilia' enables us to spread the career out further and themes, techniques, the development of a voice can be traced throughout Plath's work as a whole.

Laurence Lerner (*Encounter*, January 1982, p.53–4) sees the *Collected Poems* put together with tact and care by Ted Hughes, commenting, 'she was one of the most remarkable poets of her time'. Looking at the 1961 poem 'The Mirror' he comments on the 'verbal sprightliness', the amusing self-importance given to the mirror and how the poem relates to the wilder, tougher 'Lady Lazarus' and 'Fever 103', seeping back to the 'terrible intensity' of the *Ariel* poems yet inviting comparisons and awareness. Lerner tracks self-aware performative humour in the 'wide and incoherent outpouring of terror and self-hatred' which he notes *seems* to dominate 'Lady Lazarus'.

In recognising technical tautness and control in the later poems, humour, role play as performance and continuities of concern between earlier and later poems, Lerner begins to dispel the myths that confine criticism of Plath merely to the 'mad, hysterical female category. Lerner comments in 'Lady Lazarus' on: 'The use of repetitions that capture the frenzy of the speaking voice and find a pattern in it, and above all through the deliberate self-dramatisiation represents suicide as a form of role-playing, almost of comedy.' He finds her a performer, self-aware, blackly comic.

A broader view

One of the most influential informed works on Sylvia Plath is Anne Stevenson's *Bitter Fame* (Vintage, London, 1989). Stevenson, herself an acclaimed poet, brings together critical insights on Plath's poetry and testimony on her life from colleagues and friends, aided by Olwyn Hughes, Plath's sister-in-law. What emerges is a carefully drawn picture of a 'volatile', intense character, 'vivacious', 'stimulating', 'humorous', 'brilliant' but also 'self-absorbed, stubbornly ambitious'. The book explores established myths and new versions of Plath's life and art, showing her as contradictory and exploring her diverse reception.

The debate continues

As we have already seen, the critics have diverse views of Plath and her work. This diversity is ever growing as her work is re-evaluated and as Ted Hughes' role in her life is re-examined.

The Spectator (2000) review which received the publication of the complete Plath journals with a vitriolic response, condemning Plath as both very ordinary and very hysterically excessive seems a product of youthful intellectual spite. By way of contrast, Anne Stevenson recognises in the ordinariness of Plath's life the (professionally very dangerous) construction of her poetry for such a large readership. Like many of us, she sought individuality, identity. Her fertile mind finds patterns and meaning in her life of straight A grades and managing children. Her life might be 'ordinary' but she is a 'born poet', Stevenson argues.

Sylvia Plath rushed her moods and experiences into words and *this was* a dangerous act; it pushed her feelings into extremes, crystallised the thoughts and experiences into a perfect form, made it real. Stevenson sees Plath's urges for perfection, purging, guilt and purity running throughout her poetry. She charts in detail Plath's last few months, writing in the friends who supported her, absent from the myth and representing someone who had written herself into a corner, into a personal, performative version of a myth that eventually required her own death.

Stevenson explores and explains a great deal, pointing out a reader's personal danger in coming too close to empathy with a mind producing such fits of depression and writing at a rush.

Jacqueline Rose's *The Haunting of Sylvia Plath* (Virago, London, 1991), a new feminist view, gives us a Plath who does not need to be resolved into a single reading. Rose negotiates the treacherous rather than the biographical and even psychotic reading Plath's work has attracted. Her own psychological/ feminist/ broader view and interpretation, particularly of Plath's representations of sexuality, were the subjects of attempts to silence the work.

Olwyn and Ted Hughes called this an 'evil' book. It locates some of the readings of Plath, notably the 'schizophrenia overview' Holbrook reading, as liable to project visions of a deadly or self-destructive femininity (a male and cultural construct and myth) or feminist readings which figure Plath as victim of patriarchy and men.

Suffering the fate of women writers more broadly, then, Plath is seen by many as a poetess, cultivating her 'hysteria', victim, porn object, pornographer, showing her wares (her death).

Gilbert and Gubar's feminism focuses on expression of *identity* for women and a cosmic 'I'. Rose condemns *both* versions as refusing women's history. Rose argues that Plath's use of words is paramount. She is a poet not *merely* a person. The body is projected through words but *also* wards off phobias/ language by projecting or interjecting what disgusts, terrifies, what challenges identity and wards off fear (p.34).

✳✳✳✳SUMMARY ✳✳✳✳

- Many recent critics concentrate on a feminist version of Plath or look at all her work as indications of her death

- More balanced views have emerged in the 1990s.

What next?

9

READ MORE PLATH

Some of the further reading you could do would include a close look at the rest of Plath's *Collected Poems* and the full texts of *Letters Home*, *Johnny Panic and the Bible of Dreams* and *Journals 1959–1962*.

Also worth reading is Plath's book for children *The Bed Book* (Faber & Faber, 1976) illustrated by Quentin Blake. With Plath's reputation as a tragic, gifted, suicide, it is far too easy to forget her humour, black humour though it is, and her delight in her children. *The Bed Book* is a rhyming catalogue of desirable beds and draws from Lewis Carroll and Edward Lear, for their legacy of nonsense verse. The verse also has affinities with the Mersey Press, in particular Roger McGough or the nonsense of the Beatles in 'Yellow Submarine' (both after her time). Blake's illustrations aptly pick up the ideas of alternative beds such as: 'A Bed for Fighting', 'A Bed for Cats', 'A Bed for a Troupe of Acrobats'.

The Bed Book shows her to be in tune with the amusing and dark side of her own nature.

TED HUGHES AND *BIRTHDAY LETTERS*

So much speculation about the lives of Hughes and Plath can be somewhat answered by Hughes' publication of *Birthday Letters* just before his death in 1998. These poems fill in some details of the years he was with Plath and his feelings of loss, the clarity he brings to his understanding of her effect and intent on him. They are also poignant, sensitive, poetic love letters. Hughes identifies Plath's compulsive, driven feeling for a figure to replace or represent her father, finding this in Hughes following an arrow-straight quest.

In 'The Shot' Hughes recognises:

> Your worship needed a God.
> Where it lacked one, it found one.
>
> …
>
> Your Daddy had been aiming you at God
> When his death touched the tragic

Her Daddy, hid behind *him*, the husband who became the immediate target, being left, in echo of 'Daddy' only with tokens, reminders:

> … I managed
> A wisp of your hair, your ring, your watch, your nightgown
>
> ('The Shot', 1998, pp.16–17)

He talks of the sense of loss of the years without her, their daughter asking:

> Daddy, where's Mummy?

In *Birthday Letters* we see Plath as a victim, as an American abroad in a fever, a poem parallel to her own 'Fever 103°'.

Indiana University holds the full manuscript of *Letters Home* which were selected by her mother, Aurelia Plath. The 1982 edition of the *Journals* was edited by her husband, Ted Hughes. These original Journal extracts are highly selective, removing the embarrassing, the intimate and the perhaps cruel comments about other people. Feminist critics have particularly queried such editing. Dee Horne's article, 'Biography in Disguise: Sylvia Plath's Journals' (*Wascana Review*, 1992, 27:1 pp.90–104) compares the full to the edited texts, highlighting omissions now restored in the 2000 publication.

SUSAN BASSNETT

Susan Bassnett's brief but accessible study *Sylvia Plath* (Macmillan, London, 1987) provides an introduction to themes such as family and identity and discusses several key poems. Bassnett takes a chronological approach to Plath's work in the early part of the book and outlines key events in her life that fuelled poetic developments, making Plath accessible. Robyn Marsack's *Sylvia Plath* (Open University Press, Buckingham, 1992) provides useful information in the form of an upgraded, teaching text taking you easily through some of Plath's most complex poems, asking stimulus questions. It provides a general overview of the different critical approaches, putting her work in perspective, discussing her relationship to other confessional Americans, such as Lowell, Snodgrass, Berryman, Anne Sexton and different responses to her work through time. Some critics become embroiled in the complexity of the imagery and symbolism. Axelrod's *Sylvia Plath, The Woman and the Cure* (Johns Hopkins Press, Baltimore and London, 1990) represents her as extremely complex, impenetrable.

ROBERT LOWELL AND ANNE SEXTON
Also worth reading are the poems of Robert Lowell and Anne Sexton, the American confessional poets. Contemporaries and friends of Plath, each writes about the intersection of their lives with history. Both also, sadly, committed suicide.

Lowell, Robert (1987) *Collected Prose.* London: Faber and Faber
Lowell, Robert (1956) *For the Union Dead.* London: Faber and Faber
Sexton, Anne (1981) *The Complete Poems.* Boston: Houghton Mifflin

EMILY DICKINSON, THEODORE ROETHKE, PABLO NERUDA
Read also the poetry of Emily Dickinson, Theodore Roethke and Pablo Neruda for their influences on the younger Plath. Dickinson is a transcendentalist woman poet who writes of self, love, identity, God, death and was a recluse. Neruda's imagery and capturing of the intersection of the self and political history influenced Plath.

Dickinson, E. and Johnson, T.H. (1988) *The Complete Poems of Emily Dickinson.* New York: Little Brown and Company
Dickinson, E. and Reeves, James (1959) *Selected Poems of Emily Dickinson.* Portsmouth: Heinemann

Neruda, Pablo (1969) *Twenty Love Poems and Songs of Despair.*
  London: Cape
Roethke, Theodore (1968) *The Collected Poems of Theodore Roethke.*
  London: Faber and Faber
Roethke, Thoedore (1961) *Words for the Wind.* Indiana University
  Press, Indiana

THE INTERNET

There are also several Internet sites which have details, reviews and essays on Plath. This information was correct in 2001 but please be aware that these sites come and go and may not still be available.

The following two sites hold essays on Sylvia Plath and on Anne Sexton:

http://www.sapphireblue.com/writing/plath.html
http://acker.cwrl.utexasedu/slatin/sexton/sexton.html

The interview with Peter Orr and further student and academic essays is at:

http://ilabws.informatik.uni-leipzig.de/~beckmann/
plath/orrinterview.html

The Gale Literary Database entry for Plath is at:

http://ilabws.informatik.uni-leipzig.de/~beckmann/plath/annas.html

A selected bibliography appears at:

http://www.csustan.edu/english/reuben/pal/chap10/plath.html

Glossary

Alliteration is the repetition of the consonant, for example, 's' or 't' to gain special rhythmical or musical effects.

Assonance is the repetition of a vowel, for example, 'ee', 'a', to produce a particular effect.

Bildungsroman A German originated word, used to mean the story of an individual's life. Famous examples in fiction are *Jane Eyre, Oliver Twist, Portrait of the Artist as a Young Man.*

Constructedness refers to the socially prescribed nature of meanings that are placed on words and concepts. Women's roles are seen to be constructed because they are what society has imposed.

Cultural materialism The study of historical material within a politicised framework such as Marxism.

Diachronic Looking at the self or a work of art over a period of time, as a historic development.

End-stopped Where the sense of a line of poetry is completed at the end of the line.

Enjambement A poetry term referring to lines in poetry where the sense runs on from one line to the next.

Feminism The study of gender politics from a female perspective. Usually the term is applied to the political and social movement which swept Western Europe and the United States beginning in the late 1960s.

Gothic is the term linked to gothic architecture and used to describe a stylised form which uses elements of the sinister and grotesque, usually to create claustrophobic settings and situations. Mary Shelley's *Frankenstein* is a gothic novel and includes all the elements including old castles and a sense of darkness and danger, all wrapped up with a hint of Romanticism.

Ideology A set of beliefs (ideas), systematised so that it applies to a class or individual, often as a basis of some economic or political theory or system.

L'écriture féminine   The belief that there is a particular kind or kinds of writing specific to women in terms of expression, imagery, tone, as well as subject matter and writing of 'the body'. This is a critical belief that women write through and of their bodies. The fact that they are also bodies in the world affects the way they see, feel, experience and also express themselves. This perception will be different from those of men.

Marxist historicism   A branch of cultural materialism which analyses texts using the ideas of Karl Marx.

Mein Kampf   This was Hitler's polemical work which set out his intentions to conquer the world.

Modernism   A term used to describe the literary movement of the 1890s–1940s whose international writers numbered among them T.S. Elliot, Virginia Woolf, James Joyce and Ezra Pound. They wanted to write in a new way, rejecting the tired conventions of the nineteenth century and wished to 'make it new'. Complex technically, they often concentrated on disillusionment, fragmentation and a search for something to believe in.

New Criticism   A movement from the 1930s to the 1960s which became academic orthodoxy. It concentrated, at least at first, on short poems and sought to consider them as self-sufficient objects, disconnected from their origin and author. The idea was to discover the ambiguities and complexities found in a poem and to seek ways of resolving them in their own terms.

Nihilism   The belief that life is devoid of meaning, usually coupled with a denial of religious belief or moral principles. The predominant mode in literature is a sense of despair.

Performative   Where the language used actually performs the deed to which it refers. In Plath's case, where she explores the 'performances' required by women's roles through the language which describes it.

Psycho-biographical   In literature this is interpreting an artist's work as an index of their mental state and reading their mental state as a way of interpreting the work.

Romanticism   A movement in Britain and Europe roughly between 1770 and 1848. In literary terms it expressed the self and the value of individual experience along with a strong sense of the transcendental. The motif of the movement was 'imagination' and it had a belief in the close links between man and nature. The movement is characterised by such writers as Rousseau, Wordsworth, Mary Wollstonecraft, Coleridge, Byron and Shelley.

Edmund **Spenser** was a poet writing during the time of Queen Elizabeth I. 'Epithalamion' was a bridal celebration.

Structuralism   Intellectual movement originating in France in the 1950s in the work of Levi Straus and Roland Barthes.

Stresses that things cannot be understood in isolation but need to be seen in a wider context.

Synchronic   Looking at something as being closely attached to its time with no historic influences.

Chronology of major works

1960   *The Colossus and Other Poems*, published by Heinemann, London

1963   *The Bell Jar*, published by Heinemann, London

1965   *Ariel*, published by Faber and Faber, London

1965   *Uncollected Poems*, published by Turret Press, London

1971   *Crossing the Water*, published by Faber and Faber, London

1971   *Winter Trees*, published by Faber and Faber, London

1975   *Letters Home*, ed. Aurelia Plath, published by Harper & Row, New York

1977   *Johnny Panic and The Bible of Dreams and other prose writings*, published by Faber & Faber, London

1981   *Collected Poems*, ed. Ted Hughes, published by Faber and Faber, London

1982   *The Journals of Sylvia Plath*, eds Ted Hughes and Frances McCullough, published by The Dial Press, New York

2000   *The Journals of Sylvia Plath 1950–1962*, published by Faber and Faber, London

Index